Language in American Life

Proceedings of the Georgetown University–
Modern Language Association Conference
October 6–8, 1977, Washington, D.C.

Y0-AGT-476

E. Michael Gerli
James E. Alatis
Richard I. Brod
Editors

Georgetown University Press, Washington, D.C. 20057

Library of Congress Cataloging in Publication Data

Georgetown-Modern Language Association Conference on
    Language in American Life, Georgetown University,
    1977.
    Language in American Life.

    1. Language and languages--Study and teaching--
United States--Congresses.   I. Gerli, E. Michael.
II. Alatis, James E.   III. Brod, Richard I.
IV. Georgetown University, Washington, D. C.
V. Modern Language Association of America. VI. Title.
P57. U7G44 1977   407'.1073   78-14218
ISBN 0-87840-300-0

International Standard Book Number: 0-87840-300-0

CONTENTS

FOREWORD

The Georgetown-Modern Language Association Conference on Language in American Life was conceived by James E. Alatis, Dean of the School of Languages and Linguistics of Georgetown University, and Richard I. Brod, Director of Foreign Language Programs at the MLA. Sensing the arrival of a critical moment in the future of language education in the United States, they set out to bring together in one place the major forces of interest advocating renewed emphasis on languages in this country. As a member of the MLA committee which drafted <u>Foreign Language Programs for the Seventies</u>, Dr. Alatis was quick to point out the necessity of a new, broader, more ecumenical definition of language and its role in our society. Richard Brod's conversations with the officials of government agencies, members of the legislative branch, heads of service organizations, and leaders in the private sector had led him to the same conclusions. The Conference was therefore devised in order to initiate a dialogue between the scholarly community, the traditional proponent of the importance of language study, and the groups outside academe expressing a desire to emphasize the role of language in a world that was becoming socially, politically, and economically increasingly interdependent.

Once the need for the Conference was recognized, the task of identifying, organizing, and bringing together the divers individuals and groups who could play a part in calling attention to the importance of languages in the national life was begun. The coordinators for the Conference were Richard Brod and E. Michael Gerli, an Associate Professor in the School of Languages and Linguistics, and starting in January, 1977, they began to plan a program and contact potential speakers. The response was overwhelmingly enthusiastic. There was not only an interest but a great eagerness to participate in what many felt was a long overdue effort. The result, of course, was a vital, productive encounter attended by over 500 people representing the professional organizations, universities from all over the United

States and Canada, government officials, educators, planners, students, experts in foreign affairs and business, and a host of other individuals interested in sharing their views and committed to bringing renewed attention to the role of language in American life.

In the nearly year-long effort of organizing the Conference, the Coordinators called upon the talents and advice of numerous friends and colleagues to whom thanks should be expressed. Grateful appreciation is especially extended to James E. Alatis, Dean of the School of Languages and Linguistics, Georgetown University; and William D. Schaefer, Executive Director of the Modern Language Association. Their steadfast interest in the project was instrumental in bringing it to fruition. Moreover, thankful recognition is expressed to the speakers and workshop leaders who so willingly and generously gave of their time and of themselves in order to make the Conference a success. Sincere gratitude is owed also to the staff of the School of Languages and Linguistics for their help in the planning, especially to Mrs. Elizabeth A. Johansen, Executive Assistant to the Dean. And finally, grateful acknowledgment must be accorded Professor Richard J. O'Brien, S. J., Director and General Editor of the Publications Department of the School of Languages and Linguistics, and his staff, for dealing with the editing and technical problems of producing these proceedings.

E. Michael Gerli
School of Languages and Linguistics
Georgetown University

INTRODUCTION

The Georgetown-MLA Conference on Language in American Life owes its origin to a growing awareness on the part of America's political and educational leadership of the need for developing and expanding the international dimension of American education--involving improved information about the world, on the one hand, and greater attention to training for cross-cultural sensitivity, on the other. (Language, needless to say, both as a tool and as an object of study, can contribute to both objectives.) An important landmark in the movement to strengthen international education was the publication in 1975 of the report of the American Council on Education's International Education Project: Education for Global Interdependence. The same year witnessed the signing of the Final Act of the Conference on Security and Cooperation in Europe, the so-called Helsinki Agreement, with its strong emphasis on human rights and its less famous, though equally eloquent assertion of the intention of the participating nations to

> . . . encourage the study of foreign languages and civilizations
> as an important means of expanding communication among
> peoples for their better acquaintance with the culture of each
> country, as well as for the strengthening of international
> cooperation; . . . to stimulate . . . the further development
> and improvement of foreign language teaching and the di-
> versification of choice of languages taught at various levels
> . . .

Drawing upon the work of the American Council on Education and other agencies, the U.S. Congress in 1976 passed the so-called 'citizen education' amendment to the National Defense Education Act, with the purpose of fostering a wider application of international education in schools, undergraduate programs, and adult education.

Later that year, the joint Congressional Commission on Security and Cooperation in Europe turned its attention to the Foreign Languages and Civilizations section of the Helsinki Final Act, noting with distress both the well-documented recent decline in language enrollments in schools and colleges and the concomitant lack of competent specialists in a number of politically and economically important languages. Finally, in mid-1977 one member of the Commission, Representative Paul Simon of Illinois, led his colleagues in addressing a letter to President Carter requesting the appointment of a short-term Presidential Commission on Language and International Studies as the first stage in a process of defining national priorities in these areas.

By 1977, then, the time seemed ripe for a redefinition of the role of language study in education, with emphasis on both humanistic and practical applications of language competence. The need for such redefinition was felt, on the one hand, by language teachers, whose once secure role in school and college curriculum had been challenged by pressures for 'relevance', variously defined; and on the other hand by students, who were the victims, as it were, of the failure of their teachers to respond adequately to such pressures. What was clear, however, was that in the years since the National Defense Education Act was passed, the role of education itself had shifted and expanded. To the planners of the Georgetown-MLA Conference, traditional and specialized definitions seemed too narrow; as a framework for discussion, nothing less than 'American life', in all its diversity and complexity, seemed appropriate.

The plan of the Georgetown Conference was both modest and ambitious: modest in the sense that the theme was practical and down-to-earth; ambitious to the extent that the Conference attempted to bring together the divergent interests of scholars, teachers, students, and users of language education. Time, place, and personnel were all auspiciously chosen. The Conference took place at the beginning of an academic year (and for federal employees, a fiscal year) that saw a number of promising initiatives, among them the Task Forces project organized by the Modern Language Association and the American Council of Learned Societies, and the preparations for the expected Presidential Commission on Language and International Studies. It was also fortunate that the Conference took place in the same week as the twentieth anniversary of the launching of the first Soviet Sputnik, a fact duly noted in Washington newspapers. In fact, the event marked the beginning of a period of active and beneficial interest on the part of the media in matters involving language and language study.

The location of the Conference was also wisely chosen: not the carpeted halls of an impersonal hotel, but the living, breathing, student-occupied campus of a distinguished urban university, and specifically its nationally renowned School of Languages and Linguistics.

Speakers and workshop leaders with a wide range of occupations--
congressmen, government officials, administrators, scholars,
teachers--brought a wide range of expertise, including linguistics,
psychology, government, foreign affairs, language education, and
student guidance. At the same time, most of the leading professional
organizations were represented: not only the Modern Language
Association, as co-sponsor of the event, but also the American Council on the Teaching of Foreign Languages, represented by several of
its leaders and members; the American Association of Teachers of
Spanish and Portuguese, represented by its President; the American
Philological Association; the Linguistic Society of America; and the
organization of Teachers of English to Speakers of Other Languages.

Given these multiple purposes, audiences, and sources, the Conference could in many respects be regarded as a festival or rally: a
festival in celebration of language and language education; and a rally
in support of various initiatives to promote language study in the
United States, especially the initiatives of benevolent 'outsiders' like
Leon Panetta, Paul Simon, and Frederick Starr. It was the hope of
its planners that the Conference would not only succeed in serving
these purposes by informing, enlightening, and bringing together its
participants, but that it would also eventually be seen as the starting
point of an era of renewed interest and revitalized activity in language teaching and learning in the United States. The responsiveness
of the participants, and the fervor of their discussion, furnished evidence of the Conference's impact upon the 500 teachers, students, and
friends of language study who were present at its sessions. Its impact upon future education will be measured in the ideas and concrete
projects that are developed within and outside the language teaching
profession during the closing years of this decade.

Richard I. Brod
Modern Language Association
of America

FIRST PLENARY SESSION
INTRODUCTION

JAMES E. ALATIS
Dean, School of Languages and Linguistics
Georgetown University

Good evening, ladies and gentlemen, and welcome to the Georgetown University-Modern Language Association Conference on Language in American Life.

I have the pleasure this evening of introducing to you three distinguished speakers who will offer their views on language and its relation to civilization, education, and cultural training.

The first speaker this evening is The Reverend Timothy S. Healy, S. J., President of Georgetown University. Father Healy was awarded an A. B. degree in English literature from Woodstock College in 1946, and his Ph. D. in English from Oxford University in 1965. He also holds degrees in sacred theology and philosophy. President Healy is a Donne scholar, has published widely both on literature and education, and has served on a number of commissions dealing with education.

Our second speaker, Dr. William D. Schaefer, who will speak to us on 'Language and education', is Executive Director of the Modern Language Association. Dr. Schaefer took his B. A. in English at New York University in 1957, his M. S. from the University of Wisconsin in 1958, and his Ph. D. from the same university in 1962. He has been Associate Professor of English at Brooklyn College, and Professor of English and Department Chairman at the University of California at Los Angeles.

The final speaker this evening is Congressman Leon E. Panetta (16th District, California), whose topic is 'Language and cultural training'. Mr. Panetta received his B. A. magna cum laude from the University of Santa Clara in 1960 and graduated from the University of Santa Clara Law School in 1963.

1

I am happy to present to you Father Healy, who will begin this conference with a paper entitled 'Language and civilization'.

LANGUAGE AND CIVILIZATION

TIMOTHY S. HEALY, S. J.
President, Georgetown University

It is a pleasure to be here with you, even though it makes me feel
vaguely nervous. In a sense, speaking tonight is like returning to my
first love, except that I have not seen the lady for years, time has
taken its toll of teeth and torso, and I may not recognize her nor she
me. In fact, were I to be completely honest, the lack of recognition
might be a relief.

All that means is, I am enormously conscious that anything that I
can say tonight will be strictly introductory. Once a week I sit down
at a breakfast table and read modern English poets with a dozen medical students. They need the poetry and I need the prophylaxis. It has
been a long time since I walked into any real classroom, and an even
longer one since I walked in to teach a foreign language. I shall thus
leave the serious comments to pros like Bill Schaefer and Congressman Panetta. For myself, Dean Alatis asked me to give a generic
introduction, and I will try to do just that.

First of all, I ought to identify myself, so that you will have some
effective control on my prejudices. I am a Jesuit who has spent six
years learning Latin and five years learning Greek. The principal
parts of my education occurred at the University of Louvain and at
Oxford. I have spent most of my life teaching English, and a bit of it
teaching Latin. I am thus as perfect a specimen of an unreconstructed
(and unrepentant) liberal-artser as anyone is likely to find.

I do, however, bring to my task tonight several more immediate
qualifications. First of all, I have managed over the course of fifty
years to learn three languages. I learned two of them by immersion
(also known as 'learn or starve to death', and I learned one by teaching it. I began with Caesar and worked through to Virgil, and by the

3

end of three years, no matter what my classes had or had not learned,
I had learned some Latin.

The second qualification that I bring this evening is my lifelong
fascination with languages. Learning them was fun, using them was
even more fun. I am one of those odd people who actually learned
French by reading Larousse, and I still read the Oxford English
Dictionary for pleasure. One of the great pleasures is telling your
friends mysterious things to look up, and for those of you in the
audience who have never met anyone who told you to go to the OED
and look up the word tappen, a great discovery lies in store.

My final qualification is that I have lived through some of American higher education's stormiest years, and have spent most of those
years reflecting on colleges and storms and studies.

In the university world in which I grew up, so many things were
taken for granted. One knew what a college was, one had a firm
grasp on what a curriculum was, and the curriculum, if not revelled
in by students, was at least accepted. The college of those days was
a delight to live in. All the processes of discussion, government,
growth, and change were profoundly democratic. That meant that
we were as slow and as stupid as the weakest of our members. We
were, however, respectful of each of them. Under the decent shelter
of corporate anonymity, our idiosyncracies, crotchets, and downright
cussedness were not only tolerated but actually fostered. Perhaps the
essential ingredient of this kind of tolerance was that the college
stood in opposition to the bustling, swiftly growing republic around
it. It reserved to itself the right to criticize its own, and it trans-
ferred that right to no outsider. The result was an institution, both
tolerant and critical, which knew where it was going far better than
it knew how to get there, but in the anarchy of its heart was totally
unafraid.

What happened to tear this simple world apart? That question
reminds me of the old joke about the man who went into the drug store
to ask, 'What do you do for bee stings on poison ivy on sunburn?'
Higher education in America has had to deal simultaneously with an
earthquake, a tornado, and a flood at the same time that American
society around it has changed more than at any time in the republic's
history.

The earthquake shook out a whole value structure. The automatic
assumption of values that tied higher education together, that could
make specifically distinct institutions like Harvard and Ohio State
recognizable to a faculty member who moved from one to the other,
collapsed in the 1960s. John Donne's words, 'all cohaerence gone',
describe quite adequately what happened to the curriculum. We lost
all sense of shape, all sense of form, and jettisoned almost all of
our requirements. We no longer as academics had the calm

assurance that what we were selling was worth the buying and that we and our wares were serving the republic as clearly and as sensibly as we could.

The second catastrophe that swept over us was the flood, beginning at the end of World War II. Without any sort of public announcement, and by the most draconian kind of vote, a shift in public opinion, America moved from mass to universal higher education. Instead of saying that college as in the late eighteenth century was reserved for the aristocracy, or that as in the nineteenth century it was available to a limited but expanding number, the mid-twentieth century decided that higher education should simply be available to every citizen who wanted it. By the way, about that flood, I really am an optimist. I think it may have left more enriching minerals in our drenched soil than it brought damage to our antiquated structures.

The final explosion, all we needed to do us in, was a tornado, the victory of wind and rhetoric over civility. Within a mere decade we reduced ourselves to the kind of warring intransigence which the academic world had not seen since the Reformation. The rhetoric of entrenchment, violence, and downright brutality flourished until we drowned in it and passed from word to act. Civility is a thin tissue, and can at times be bloodless. It can also, at times, hide fraud, deceit, and corruption. But the notion that the uncivil is somehow uncivilized is something to which we had best return with all deliberate speed. I have a private nightmare of what happens when a whole profession forgets that underneath all the crying of wolf, there may actually lurk a wolf.

Amid all those changes I would like this evening to single out only one. That is the disruption of the curriculum to a point where it no longer mattered what a student learned, provided that the very best of the breed were prepared for a Ph.D. and the devil took the hindmost. We came in the late sixties and early seventies to the point where it was conceded that no one could any longer cope with all of Western society. Instead of trying to figure out what elements one had to cope with in order to survive in that same society, we decided that if our intellectual world was all chards and orts, our offerings to our students could be the same. And for those students who could not cope with the ambiguity of a Horn and Hardart Cafeteria we created a McDonald's--the professional school with only one offering, variously dressed and seasoned.

One of the elements of the curriculum which was abandoned with all deliberate speed was the study of foreign languages, including the classical ones. It had been traditional in American colleges to insist on certain foreign language preparation before college entrance. That died first, and almost immediately afterwards the colleges themselves began dropping their requirements for any kind of linguistic competence other than English. There is some evidence on the landscape that they have also dropped English, but that is not the subject of this conference.

American education has always had trouble with foreign languages for a variety of reasons, some of them honest. The first is our relative isolation. One has to travel a long distance even from outer America (let alone from middle America) before finding a foreign language to speak. Even to the north of us, French is an embattled minority. The only Americans who had ready access to a foreign language were the residents of the Southwest.

We of course share the arrogance of great nations, which makes it difficult for them to adapt either to the language or the ways of others. The greatest example of this in Europe is France. George Bernard Shaw's comment, 'The French don't care what you do as long as you pronounce it properly', while an amusing moral reflection, is one of the principal hazards that the foreigner encounters. In addition to this arrogance which we share with France and England and Germany, we in America have a specific one. We take it for granted that all foreigners want to become Americans, as quickly as possible. The fact that some of them might not want to do so, and want rather to persist in their benighted ways, as well as to speak their ridiculous local dialect, strikes all of us as first a surprise and secondly a shame. We have learned since the late nineteenth century to leave them in the errors of their ways if they insist upon them. That does not change our own opinion of the process.

Finally, of course, languages are difficult, and difficult subjects in the curriculum, unless they are seen as essential to some immediate reward or unless, as in the sciences, they make part of a brick wall which must be erected brick by brick, are the first to go. It is interesting that the first warning signal that there were serious academic difficulties in American secondary education was the steady collapse of skill in foreign languages and mathematics. More and more the colleges had to water down the content of their language courses until they began language instruction in freshman year and hoped that in a year or a year and a half a student could catch up and devote himself to the literary and other studies which had previously been considered college work. This process, however, had its own drawbacks. Students found the work demeaning and too reminiscent of high school, and when given the option, opted out of languages in droves. Too much language instruction had to do with basics, and basics are, as they have always been, boring.

The personal results of this whole process were of course only too predictable. The first was a weakening of the grasp and control of the English language. It is hard to deal with the complexities of English grammar when one starts from no place else. Professor

Masciantonio will demonstrate to us that there is a direct line between the abandonment of foreign languages and the weakening in one's control of English. This weakening can go beyond sloppy grammar. One can work at the gradual evisceration of language, until it consists of the kind of empty idiocies which someone has defined as phatic. Unless, for example, one has learned some Latin, or at least a Latin language, one cannot appreciate how fully the Latinate form and the Latinate word in English are essentially the language of lies. I used to tell freshmen classes that no red-blooded American male or female in his or her right mind ever told someone to fornicate hence. There were splendid Anglo-Saxon monosyllables to convey that message in much more forcible terms.

As an example of linguistic deterioration, consider the object that rests in the back pocket of every airplane seat. When I first traveled by air in the 1930s, if one took it out, there was mimeographed on the side of it the blunt identification, vomit bag. Immediately after the Second World War, that homely object had been transmuted by the alechemy of commercial ignorance of language into an air sickness bag. That was of course a degradation, but at least two of the words were Anglo-Saxon. You can imagine my dismay to find some months ago that the same object, in the same position in the aircraft, is now called a motion discomfort receptacle. People who describe a vomit bag as a motion discomfort receptacle belong on everybody's fecal roster.

Ambassador de Madariaga may sometimes exaggerate, but he does point up a second personal loss which lack of language instruction has brought to us. That is the loss of the capacity to proceed beyond linguistic structures and beyond the cultural dimensions which they carry with them. Old William of Wyckham should really have written over his college gates, 'language maketh man', because in so many deep ways it does. The man who is tied to only one linguistic structure has really lost one of the greatest chances to grow beyond and outside of himself.

Once foreign language studies are abandoned, every other literary, historical, or philosophical subject in the curriculum must suffer. I was appalled to find in the 1960s that graduate students in Oxford, working in Renaissance English literature, could not cope with such simple Latin as that found in the Glossa Ordinaria. Obviously, one can get through life without reading the Glossa Ordinaria. But if one is working in the Renaissance, it really seems to me that to be ignorant of Latin is to be out of the running. That is a personal example, but I suspect all of us could come up with equally bad memories. In my own field, how one understands the romantics without knowing German, the eighteenth century without knowing French, or Chaucer without knowing Latin, leaves me deeply puzzled. The answer is, I think, that one really understands none of them.

Let me again, in a purely personal aside, indicate what I feel to be a fourth loss, the deprivation of all our students of something I have found a marvelous joy. That is watching the intricate and fluid gears of the mind shift from language to language, change pace and rhythm, walk from one proud and lovely structure into another, and enjoy the process enormously. To pass from the Old Vic doing Shakespeare to the Comédie Française doing Molière, is to walk from Windsor to Versailles, from one marvelous corner of the mind to another, from one world into another, and above all from one rhythm and pace into another. All of these changes depend on the magic of language, and without that magic, all of them are lost.

If the personal losses due to our national abandonment of languages are serious, and if they must inevitably weaken the collegiate career of every student who suffers them, the social results are perhaps even more drastic. Edmund Burke once remarked that great empires and little minds go ill together. One wonders really, in the late adventures of this republic, whether or not the fact that only a handful in the United States could read or speak Vietnamese had more to do with our terrible involvement in that tiny country than almost any other aspect of our national ignorance. I am also tempted to feel that part of our trouble in Vietnam was our incapacity to read Greek, because Thucydides, in recounting the expedition to Syracuse, told us exactly what happens to people who go to war in the wrong place, for the wrong reason, a very long way from home. But surely, at least part of our terrible insensitivity in all our dealings in Asia has been that so few of us can cope with the subtlety and the beauty of Asian language.

The isolation goes deeper, however, than our ears and tongues. It is really an isolation of soul. Our ignorance of language keeps us nationally from making the kind of salving contact which ties people together, which enables man to talk to man, and which can in the long run prevent embroilment, misunderstanding, and violence. It is through language that we reach deeply into the being of other people, understand their customs and their usages, share with them their joy and their sorrow, and above all, share with them ourselves. On the stairwell next to me at Oxford was a Ghanaian named Peter Sarpong. He was doing a degree in anthropology and came up before I did. A few days after I arrived he came into my room and we chatted for a while, and he asked to borrow a pencil. I gave it to him and he burst out laughing. I asked him what he was laughing at and he said that I had just been very rude. I was puzzled, and inquired what on earth he meant. He then told me that had we been in Ghana, it would have taken him fifteen minutes to build up to asking for the pencil and five minutes to build down from it. It would then have been my turn and it would have been appropriate for me to take ten minutes to build up to the granting of it, and five ceremonial minutes to cover my embarrassment at having been forced to do him a favor. I found this fun, and we kept talking, and finally he said to me, 'The trouble is your language. English is meant for doing business and in a hurry. In Ghanaian we cope with this sort of thing better.' I can remember at the moment wishing very desperately that I spoke this good and kindly man's language. I can remember, too, how hard it would have been for me to gain this insight into the ritual spaciousness of African life had he not spoken mine.

That personal aside hides for me the spectre of an enormous danger for these United States. We have long been famous for advertising the arrogance of our ignorance of other peoples' ways and customs. The time has now come, in the enormous interdependence of our days, when that advertisement is an insult beyond bearing. It is an insult for which we will pay deeply, and over and over again.

To the extent that we as a nation are incapable of reaching other men in other lands, of talking across our differences no matter how terrible, no matter how vast, to that extent we fulfill the awful image of Auden's Ogre. This Ogre was invented to honor the Russian invasion of Czechoslovakia. It could have come stalking out of our own conduct in Vietnam. It could also be a terrible epitaph for a nation of enormous power that could not speak to its neighbors:

> The Ogre does what ogres can,
> Deeds quite impossible for Man,
> But one prize is beyond his reach,
> The Ogre cannot master Speech.
> About a subjugated plain,
> Among its desperate and slain,
> The Ogre stalks with hands on hips,
> While drivel gushes from his lips.

It may be because I am no longer slugging it out in the day-by-day struggle of the classroom that I tend to see this academic issue in such national and international perspective. Be that as it may, it seems to me that what we are here to discuss is something of serious national interest and of major international importance. I join you in urging President Carter to move forward to create his special commission on language studies. I know that that is your wish too, and that it is essentially in support of this proposal that you are gathered here.

LANGUAGE AND EDUCATION

WILLIAM D. SCHAEFER
The Modern Language Association of America

In this my seventh year as executive director of the Modern Language Association, I have come to suspect that virtually everything there is to say about language and education has already been said, and far more effectively and with greater authority than I could ever hope to say it. In these brief remarks, I will therefore limit myself to five points involving ideas which, if not new, seem important enough to bear repeating.

1. Language and basic skills. Most language teachers would agree with the idea that the ideal time to begin learning a second language is during the elementary school years, or earlier. Indeed, many of the high hopes of the 1950s were predicated on the expectation that effective foreign language programs would soon be developed in the elementary schools. Much of today's bilingual effort is, of course, directed toward grade school children, but such programs tend to be special cases born of social need within specific locales or certain geographic regions. Currently, foreign languages are not being widely taught in the elementary schools, and, things being as they are, many of us would probably be content were we merely assured that our children are effectively being taught the English language, without worrying for the present about French or German or Spanish. Those few schools that have managed to maintain FLES programs are surely to be applauded, and we can all hope that better days lie ahead. For the foreseeable future, however, I fear that FLES will play only a limited role in language education in the United States.

I speak, however, about the teaching of specific languages and not about the teaching of language per se. The teaching of language awareness, of what might be called language sensitivity, can and should be a part of the curriculum in all schools at all grade levels. Teaching language sensitivity is not only possible but, I would argue, essential, and quite inseparable from the teaching of reading and writing in the English language. For 14 consecutive years we have witnessed a decline in SAT verbal scores, and, while recent investigations have unearthed any number of plausible reasons for the decline, I believe the primary reason is simply our declining emphasis on teaching school children about language, about how it evolves, how it functions. If we cannot teach Latin and Greek, French and German, Spanish and Russian, Chinese and Arabic to all grade school students--and I do not believe we can--surely we can at the very least teach them about other languages, and thereby instill in them a greater sensitivity to their own language and a desire some day to learn a language other than their own. I do not discount the value in teaching young people about other cultures, about other voices in other rooms, but my emphasis is on teaching about the voices themselves, language as a global phenomenon, language as the quintessential human attribute. These things are not uninteresting to the young mind; on the contrary, they are of compelling interest. We do our students and our society a tremendous disservice in ignoring them.

2. The language requirement. As we approach the 1980s, it is high time to begin to repair some of the damage done to education during the massacre of standards that occurred in the 1960s. As I read them, all the instruments agree that the time for rebuilding is upon us, for the students themselves are beginning to demand some of the rights of which we have deprived them--the right to know how to read, to know how to write, to know how to think. It is my hope, therefore, that during the next few years, high schools, colleges, and universities will restore basic requirements and, foremost among them, some kind of language requirement.

Eliminating the requirements was easy; it is not hard to destroy. To restore meaningful standards, to rebuild, is difficult, but I believe the time is ripe for mounting successful campaigns within our educational institutions. As a signatory to the Helsinki Agreement, our country has committed itself to encouraging the study of foreign languages. President Carter has commended those who are currently studying a foreign language, has encouraged other citizens to do likewise, and has agreed to appoint a commission to explore ways to strengthen and improve language study in the United States. There are, no doubt, many ways to accomplish this goal, but I suspect they all involve taking language seriously within our schools and colleges. We must approach the local school boards, the presidents and chancellors of our colleges, and must ask them what they believe to be the importance of language acquisition. If the answer is negative, if the

school or college considers languages to be of little or no importance, then we should have that stated so that everyone connected
with the particular institution will be able to act accordingly. If the
answer is that languages are of only mild importance, then let us
hear that too. But if the answer is that languages are, as President
Carter has stated, of immense importance to our country, then we
must insist that the institution take steps to ensure that language
studies receive high priority. No one can legislate a multilingual
America, but every school and college in this country can, on its own
initiative, oblige students to attain a specified level of proficiency in
at least one language other than their own. That is called a requirement, and I am for it.

3. Proficiency. The word I use, however, is 'proficiency', for,
without worrying about precise definition, I think proficiency and not
a set number of courses or of course credits should be the basis for
the language requirement. More often than not, the course requirement as used in the 1960s was a copout, enabling a school to give
the impression that a particular subject was of importance without
having to take seriously the teaching of that subject. Indeed, I believe the foreign language course requirement, more than any other
single factor, is responsible for the dismal state of languages in our
schools and colleges today. What inevitably happens is that the course
becomes the end in itself, with students forced to take no more than
a der-die-das dip at the fountain. My own academic transcript shows
two years of high school Latin, three semesters of college Spanish, a
graduate course in Old English, and successful completion of Ph. D.
exams in French and German. The transcript is, however, fraudu-
lent, for it was all a game, an obstacle course in which no meaningful
level of proficiency was ever stipulated, or anticipated, or attained.
Along with thousands of others, I der-die-das'd myself from high
school diploma to Ph. D. , passed all the course requirements, and
failed to attain proficiency in any one of the five languages I studied.
That is not the way to go. We need to stipulate a specific level of
attainment, one appropriate to the particular degree and the particular institution. However modest the goal, it must be clearly stated
and must be met, without compromise and without exception. Above
all, it must be meaningful, must ensure that the student can use the
language to the extent that it provides some degree of self-satisfaction.
That is not much to ask, but, in the final analysis, it is everything.

4. Beyond the classroom. Although I am sure we could all point
to exceptions, more often than not language education has failed in
our schools and colleges not only because we have measured out our
lives in course units (take three and see), but have failed to provide

our students with a hospitable climate in which they can use the language. I am not talking about classroom methods; I am talking about going beyond the classroom, giving students an opportunity to expand their proficiency, however modest that might be, through speaking, hearing, reading, and thus growing with the second language experience.

What we do not need is what I call the Friday afternoon Disneyland-of-the-North session--the lederhosen and the bullfight posters and the Kool-Aid in the Gallo wine bottles (Edith Piaf records in the background). That's playing games again, fine as a pedagogical gimmick in the elementary schools but not what I have in mind for secondary and postsecondary education. What we have to do is to create an environment outside of the classroom in which our students, at work or at play, can use the languages they are studying. I believe we have not begun to realize the potential in foreign exchange programs--coming and going--and that is one area where I should like to see large federal expenditures in support of the Helsinki Agreement. But we also have not begun to realize the potential within American communities for bringing foreign languages out of the closet and allowing them to occupy a meaningful place in the mainstream of our culture. Until we do, language learning in this country will continue to be an exercise in the unreal and the impractical.

5. Humanist and pragmatist. Finally, I should like to suggest that we will never reach the promised land until we recognize that both the humanistic and the pragmatic arguments for, and approaches to, language learning are valid. I need not spell out for this particular audience all that these terms involve, but I am concerned that there continues to be a certain degree of divisiveness between the area studies people and the language specialists, the literary scholars and the language pedagogues, culture and career proponents, natives and nonnatives. This is silly. The enemy is provincialism, isolationism, monolingualism, and there is no single front on which that enemy can be attacked, no single weapon with which to attack. We need them all.

To persuade the public of the importance of our concerns, we need generous federal and state support and a concerted effort involving the entire profession. We need the support of our educational institutions and of all of our colleagues, whatever their discipline, within those institutions. And, as a profession, we need to be far more effective than we have been in the past in teaching languages. There is, in brief, no panacea, no 'one thing needful'. But if we keep the end in mind and recognize that there are many different means to that end, we can all become humanistic pragmatists (or pragmatic humanists) in working together to attain the common goal.

With the support of our friends in the National Endowment for the Humanities, the State Department, the Office of Education, the Congress, and the White House, we have every reason to believe that the 1980s will see a new beginning for language study in America. Since the 1960s, the situation has deteriorated with alarming speed, and, viewed from a national perspective, it is not an exaggeration to say that today we have no place to go but up. I look forward to our doing precisely that in the months and years ahead.

LANGUAGE AND CULTURAL TRAINING

CONGRESSMAN LEON E. PANETTA
16th District, California

It is a great pleasure for me to have this opportunity to speak to you. As a product of Jesuit education, it is very comfortable to come to another Jesuit institution. As Ronald Reagan said about redwoods, 'If you've seen one, you've seen them all.' So, there is some comfort here in coming back to a Catholic university and particularly a Jesuit university.

There is also some discomfort, because frankly, I feel that on the topic of foreign language training there are people in this audience who are much more adept at the answers than I. I am reminded of the story of the nuclear physicist who won the Nobel Peace Prize. He was traveling throughout the nation, giving addresses and seminars. One day as he was traveling towards the San Joaquin Valley in California, his chauffeur leaned back over the seat and said, 'You know, Professor, I've heard that same speech so many times that I think I could give it myself.' The professor said, 'Well, I'll take you up on that. At the next stop I'll put on the chauffeur's uniform and you put on my suit and you give the speech.'

When they arrived, they exchanged clothes and the chauffeur got up and gave the speech. He gave it word for word, without any mistakes, and received a standing ovation. The professor, out in the audience, just sat there in total disbelief. Then, someone raised his hand and said, 'Professor, that was an outstanding address, but there is one thing about your formulas that bothers me.' Then he want into a question that was about three paragraphs long, with a number of formulas, equations, and technical terms, and finally said, 'Professor, what do you think about that?'

The chauffeur looked at him for a long time and then said, 'You know, that's the stupidest question I've ever heard, and to show you

16

how stupid it is I'm going to have my chauffeur answer it from out there in the audience.'

So, I am sure that as we proceed, I can point to many of you for some of the answers that we seek in this area, and do so with a great sense of relief.

I want to speak to you not so much as someone trained in foreign languages, and certainly not as one who's an expert in that area. But I do have a background that has given me a particular interest in foreign languages and cultural training.

Obviously, the name Panetta is Italian; my parents were immigrants from Italy in the early '30s. As a child I was certainly subject to cultural training, only I did not know it until I saw 'The Godfather'. So I bring to you the perspective of someone who was raised with an awareness of being an Italian, in a family where Italian was spoken. I also speak as one who was Director of the Office for Civil Rights at HEW at a time when we were beginning to break ground on the issue of discrimination against children who could not speak English, and as an attorney who handled cases involving language-based discrimination. Finally, I would like to mention some of the perspectives I see as a congressman.

There was a period in our history when we moved toward the melting pot idea, and this was felt in my family. As a child in an Italian family, my effort was not to retain that cultural identification but to blend into the society in which I was growing up. When my parents spoke Italian in front of my friends who were 'Anglos', I was embarrassed. The result was that the heritage we shared within the family was not the same one I carried outside the family. And I think this was typical of my generation. It was a period in our history when we tried to emphasize that we were all one and it was important for us to break away from what our parents had brought to this country.

Since then, I think we have begun to recognize that we really are not a melting pot; we are a diverse society in which we retain at least parts of an earlier heritage and culture, and that is good. That heritage is a key factor in establishing the sense of identity and dignity we need to deal with the rest of society. Our recognition of this point, I think, has led to a new emphasis on ethnic minorities in education and public policy. I point out to my constituents when I go home that we have a number of caucuses in the House of Representatives now. We have the Black Caucus, the Hispanic Caucus, the Northeastern Caucus, the Women's Caucus, and, yes, we now have an Italian Caucus. When I first went into the House of Representatives, the congressman from Chicago, Frank Annunzio, came up to me and said, 'Panetta, I expect that you're going to be a member of the Italian Caucus.' I said, 'Certainly', because I was not going to say no to an Italian from Chicago.

We have 35 members in the Italian Caucus. And as Mr. Annunzio says, 'We don't do much on issues, but we eat well.'

There is a new recognition, as I said, of ethnic minorities, and a new reluctance to break away from our heritage. This involves a recognition of the relationship of language to culture. Obviously, one does not understand a culture thoroughly without the ability to speak the language. When we used to invite guests to our home, it was embarrassing to hear them ask us to 'pass the paste.' At first we did not know what they were talking about.

Failure to recognize the tie between culture and language, moreover, can have much more serious consequences than social embarrassment. We have found that in elementary schools there has been built-in discrimination against children who are unable to speak English.

In the State of California not so long ago, a survey was done of children in classes for the mentally retarded. In one district over 70 percent of the children in these classes were Spanish speaking. When a careful study was made of these children, it was discovered that almost 90 percent of them were not retarded at all, but were simply unable to speak English. The schools did not take the time to deal with these children, but simply shoved them aside into the mentally retarded classes. This led to the decision in the Lau case involving Chinese children in San Francisco, in which the Supreme Court ruled that children who were unable to speak English ought to be provided bilingual teachers. Later, the Congress passed the Bilingual Education Act and provided assistance based on that act. For the first time school districts were emphasizing the need for bilingual teachers and for bilingual staff.

Now, let me mention something that is disturbing in that context, because I think there is no one here who would disagree that it is good that we provide this kind of training for those who cannot speak English. There is, as with everything that relates to civil rights or the term 'civil rights', a backlash developing in this country. I have experienced it in my district, and I am sure those of you here who are from the Southwest or the West have also experienced it. The attitude goes something like this: those children ought to be speaking English if they want to be Americans, and their families ought to be speaking English if they really want to be Americans.

Recently, I was attending the Santa Rosalia Festival in Monterey, in which the fishermen go out and bless their fleet, and an Italian came up to me there. He had a large mustache and obviously had recently arrived in this country. He said, 'Mr. Panetta, what are we going to do to stop these damn immigrants from coming in?'

Indeed, that is what I have heard in a number of areas. Constituents come up and say, 'Look, it's time that we stop the Indochinese from coming into this country. It's time we stop Orientals from coming into this country. It's time we deal with the illegal alien problem.' I am not saying that we should not be dealing with the illegal alien problem, of course. But I am disturbed when I see this issue become a basis for reacting against all immigrants. It concerns me because, indeed, our country was created and nurtured by immigration. We are a nation of immigrants. That is what the Statue of Liberty represents in the harbor of New York.

I think that kind of backlash is connected, in part, with the decline that is taking place in the study of languages. Children who should be and may even want to be studying Spanish go home and hear their parents decrying those who speak Spanish, and are turned off. We have got to deal with that. I think that if we are going to build the kind of understanding that we need in this country, we must try to make clear that the ability to speak two languages is a tremendous asset, not a burden, and that we should be advancing this idea in our society. Yes, English should be and will be our primary language, but this should not detract from the preservation or learning of a second language.

The fact that children are now not studying language as they should be leads, I think, to a number of consequences beyond the classroom. Today, one of the things we talk about in connection with foreign policy is human rights. We cannot effectively promote human rights, however, unless we wipe away the image of the 'ugly American'. The way to do that is largely through communication, and this involves the ability to speak to people in their own language.

In my district, I have what is called 'The Defense Language Institute', which is dedicated to language training for those in the military. It is a good institution, but what happens is that these students no sooner pick up the new language than they drop it. There is no followup. There is no emphasis on retention after the student leaves. I think we must emphasize the need for people in this country to have the capacity to speak a second language. From a broader perspective, it is important to the image we want to present to countries abroad and to our foreign policy, as well as to our society itself in dealing with the kind of problems that I have described.

It was for those reasons that several congressmen--Paul Tsongas, Paul Simon, and I--were all thinking about the same thing, trying to focus the attention of this country on the need to study foreign languages. Too often in government we deal with problems through crisis. The less colorful problems that we deal with on a day-to-day basis somehow are not addressed until something dramatic happens to bring them into focus. I was testifying today before the Budget Committee on my proposal to require a longer period of program oversight by the committees of the House, and the comment was, 'Well, isn't this something we should be doing anyway, without a major bill?' Of course, it is something we should be doing anyway, but it does not happen until we provide the public focus. And that is why the Commission on Foreign Languages is so important--it helps to focus the attention of the country.

A person who reads about it in his newspaper in his hometown begins to think about the problem. Paul Tsongas and I sent letters to many of you asking for your input on that, and I deeply appreciate the responses that we have received.

We are moving toward the establishment of a Foreign Languages Commission. There is no question in my mind that it is going to be created. If it is going to be effective, though, it has to be more than just an academic commission. It has to be one that gets out and truly looks at the language-related problems in education, in foreign policy, in our society in general. It must look at those problems and come up with answers and, if necessary, with legislative remedies and assistance. If it becomes just another commission in a myriad of commissions that we have created over the last few years, then it is not going to do anything and, indeed, could amount to a retreat from the problem at hand. So, it is important as that commission and its membership are announced that you participate to the maximum extent in providing direction and in making certain that it is an active commission that does not get lost in the woodwork.

The simple point I think we all make by virtue of our presence at this conference is that our heritage is, indeed, important, and that language is very much a part of that heritage, whatever it may be. But, more importantly, that language is essential to the kind of understanding we need to preserve the fabric of our society here and abroad.

So, I wish you well in your conference, and I hope that this is the beginning of a long friendship.

SECOND PLENARY SESSION
INTRODUCTION

PETER KROGH
Dean, School of Foreign Service
Georgetown University

I am most pleased to have this opportunity to preside at a discussion of language in America's international life.

The importance of language to the successful conduct of international relations would appear to be so obvious as to obviate the need for a meeting devoted to this subject. Yet in many ways the history of language teaching in the United States, so far as I have been able to observe it, has been a history of arguing a case whose self-evidence is exceeded only by the perduring popular notion that our native language will suffice for all essential purposes.

As the Washington Post reminded us this morning, this week is the twentieth anniversary of Sputnik--an event which provided a surge of spending for foreign language instruction. This spending constituted a capital investment in international literacy which we have been living off of ever since. That investment has not been renewed, yet world events since Sputnik have if anything increased the urgency of their summons to a massive national commitment to educating Americans whose language effectiveness is not limited to ease of communication in Peoria.

In summarizing the nature and implication of post-Sputnik events, Dr. Henry Kissinger, now best known as University Professor of Diplomacy at Georgetown, wrote in a recent article that 'for the first time in American history, we can neither dominate the world nor escape from it. Henceforth this country will be engaged in world affairs by reality and not by choice. America must now learn to conduct foreign policy [and here is the key phrase] as other nations have had to conduct it--with patience, subtlety, imagination, and perseverance.'

21

If Jim Alatis had got to Kissinger before he published this article he would, I am sure, have succeeded in convincing him that to these qualities should be added 'and with the ease and effect that can only come from knowing a foreign language'.

But, much as I would like it to be, my role this morning is not to make the case for the essentiality of language to America's international life--nay, to its international survival; my role is to introduce the experts who have worked for this proposition and whose professional lives have been dedicated through their role as teachers and scholars to its practical implementation.

The first of our triad of speakers is Dr. Charles Ferguson, Professor of Linguistics at Stanford University, a little known institution of higher learning on the West coast. Dr. Ferguson has a distinguished record of teaching, publication, and government service--capped by a period of service as a Visiting Professor at Georgetown in 1955. His specialty in the Arab language could not be more pertinent to the new world realities which have come to place a high premium on learning this language. Dr. Ferguson will speak on 'Language and Global Interdependence'.

Our second panelist is Wilga Rivers, Professor of Romance Language and Language Coordinator at Harvard University. Dr. Rivers is herself from an international background--born in Australia, educated in France, and professionally active in both Europe and Asia. Her books include Teaching Foreign Language Skills and Speaking in Many Tongues, something she does so well herself. Her subject this morning is 'Language and Cognition'.

Our third panelist is Dr. Harold Allen, Professor Emeritus of the English and Linguistics Department of the University of Minnesota. Dr. Allen's contributions to the language teaching and learning profession would lead one to believe that he is an institution more than an individual. His publications and professional contributions reflect a lifelong concern for the subject he addresses today, namely, 'English in Global Interdependence'.

LANGUAGE AND GLOBAL INTERDEPENDENCE

CHARLES A. FERGUSON
Stanford University

It is a pleasure to be back at Georgetown, a university where I have many associations, having taught occasional courses, partici- pated in the annual Round Tables, and worked with individual faculty members and students. It is always good to come and talk with friends at Georgetown, and I am happy with the topic I have been assigned, although I may resist the temptation to treat it in the most obvious ways. First, there is the temptation, in giving a talk of this kind, simply to repeat and elaborate statements of principles to which we all agree. We could tell ourselves that the world is getting small in terms of communication and transportation, and the problems of interaction among nations make it more urgent that we have greater command of languages. We all know that. We all accept it. We could tell ourselves that an individual does not really have any proper per- spective on the world and is severely limited in his understanding of the events around him, if he has only one language, and that it is only by the study of other languages, by really learning other languages, that we can acquire the broad perspective which is necessary in deal- ing with our immediate surroundings and the rest of the world. All of us here subscribe to that and we could talk about it at some length.

We could even remind ourselves of the fact that human language is in many ways a window on the human mind, that on the one hand it reveals to us important universal characteristics about humanity and human nature and on the other hand, it serves as a very sensitive re- flector of the profoundly different cultural values that different socie- ties have. We could say those things, which we all believe to be true, and it is a great temptation to go over that familiar territory.

A very different possibility would be to provide careful, good statistics on a number of important language questions: How many people speak which languages where, and to whom? How many people speak more than one? What nations are multilingual or monolingual? What are the actual patterns of language use in international organizations, in the reading of literature across countries or in our own everyday life? It would really be useful to have page after page of solid statistics with decimal points and percentages, with indices of language diversity and so forth, because unless we have that kind of information in some reliable, precise form, it is difficult to come to a rational understanding about language in American life or anywhere else. I hope that someday we can have access to such information in a way that we can all make use of, but I was not really tempted to present it here, partly because it is such a tough job to pull together even what reliable information is available, and also because I just do not like handling a lot of figures like that and I am not sure you would find them either fascinating or comprehensible.

So what am I going to do? I would like to take an informal look at the language situation in the world, then take an informal look at the language situation in the United States, and then ask a simple question about those two situations.

First, the language situation in the world. It is hard for us to step outside of our usual ways of looking at the world or thinking about language and to imagine that we are somehow newcomers to earth and want to characterize the use of verbal and related communication among the human species. But let's try it anyway. I suppose the first thing that we would notice after our surprise at finding a species which could communicate by making sounds would be diversity. The great invention of language itself and its basic characteristics would, no doubt, be noticed, but, once its existence were acknowledged, I think we would notice the diversity. Many languages are spoken on earth. The experts do not even know how many. Let us say there are 6,000 languages, give or take a thousand or two; it must be something on that order. We have some 6,000 different languages in the world, mutually unintelligible ways of communicating, exchanging information, giving expression to our feelings and thoughts, identifying our social group memberships, and all the other things that language does. Six thousand or so languages, plus at least 100 or so 'dead' languages, which nobody speaks as a mother tongue, but which are still being read or used in a variety of ways and have to be added to the inventory.

The diversity in language structure and language use is very great. All languages have something like verbs, but some languages regularly put the verb first, some put the verb last, and some seem to put the verb anyplace they please. All languages have consonants and vowels but some have lots of consonants and very few vowels, others have plenty of both. Some languages have nothing but monosyllables with a very limited phonetic structure, others have the most incredibly polysyllabic words. The world has five major writing systems in use: the roman alphabet of most European languages and many others, the Cyrillic alphabet of Russian and some other languages, the arabic script used for the languages of most Islamic nations, the dozen alphabets of India and South Asia, and the systems of the Chinese type. And this list does not include such interesting systems as the Hebrew alphabet which the Jews use for Hebrew, Yiddish, and other languages; the special alphabets of Ethiopia or Mongolia, or the syllabary of the Cherokee Indians in the United States. Some of these go from left to right, some from right to left, and some from top to bottom.

Great though the differences in linguistic structure and writing systems are, the diversity of use is just as great. Some languages are used only at home and their speakers would not think of using them in public or with anyone outside the family. Some languages are only used on occasions of religious significance, for public worship, private prayer, or the reciting of a ritual. Millions of people in this world use one language only for higher education and certain kinds of science and technology, and use other languages altogether in their everyday life. The list of special uses for particular languages or language varieties is very long. After noticing the fundamental fact of language and the diversity of structure and use, we might also notice that some of the world's languages are spoken by enormous numbers of people. If we just limit ourselves to languages that are somewhere in the hundred-million bracket, we might make the observation that most of the people in the world speak one of the top 11 languages. I always like to say '11' because the eleventh is French, which is too important to omit. Most of the people in the world speak one of these as their 'mother tongue' (in alphabetical order): Arabic, Bengali, Chinese, English, French, German, Hindi-Urdu, Japanese, Portuguese, Russian, Spanish.

If we all spoke all eleven of those languages, our communication problems would vanish; that is, we could speak with people just about all over the world without worrying about the other five or six thousand languages. The fact that there is a small group of very important languages in terms of number of speakers already makes a difference. And let me remind the foreign language teachers among us, specialists in literature and humanistic disciplines, that every one of those languages is also the vehicle of an important body of literature. In fact, most of the languages on the list are vehicles not only for an enormous literature, but a great, distinguished world literature. That is worth thinking about too. Of course, there are other languages than those 11 which are the vehicles of great bodies of literature, such as Persian, Italian, Old Icelandic, Latin, or Sanskrit. Nevertheless, on that list we have not only languages spoken by the greatest number of individuals as mother tongues and used for a wide variety of other purposes but also the bearers of great literatures.

If we look a little more closely, we can find the answer to another question about language. How do people communicate with other people when they do not share a mother tongue? Because, after all, that is a problem all over the earth: people have to talk to one another even though their mother tongues are different. The most common solution to the problem is to use a second language. Certain languages provide the function of a lingua franca much more than other languages, that is, they serve as a means of communication across languages. If we look at languages that way, we will have to have a somewhat different list of top languages.

Incidentally, there are many maps of languages of the world by mother tongue, but there is not a single good map of the world which shows principal lingua francas; that is, the languages you 'can get around in', the languages which people actually use to communicate across language boundaries in various parts of the world. Although Chinese may have a larger number of native speakers, English is learned by more people as a lingua franca than Chinese. This leads us to another observation about the world language situation, the special role of English. English is the language most used as a second language (or third or fourth), as a nonmother tongue for communication throughout the world, and its use is still increasing. If a Russian pilot lands in Peking he speaks to the air control people in English. That is a good symbol of the special role that English has. English is the medium of education in a number of Asian and African countries, it is the language most used at international meetings, and the most common language of scientific publication.

Finally, we might notice that the human species is broken up into a number of political units called nations, and that each nation seems to have its own pattern of language use. In America, we tend to assume that every nation has its own language and every language its nation. In fact, however, that is not the way nations work. If you think of our top 11 languages, almost every one of them is the official language of more than one nation. This is obviously true of English, Spanish, and Arabic, each of which is used officially by a score or more nations. Bengali is official in both India and Bangladesh, Portuguese in Portugal, Brazil, Mozambique, and elsewhere, and so on down the list. Some nations are very homogeneous in language, almost everybody speaking the same language. In other nations almost no two people seem to speak the same language. Some multilingual nations forbid the public use of local languages, others encourage it. In some nations the language question is highly politicized, in others it is taken for granted.

Well, we have not done justice to the picture of language use in the world, but we have at least taken an informal look at the total language situation on earth. Now let's look at the language situation in the United States.

The most striking fact is the dominance of English. In a meeting like this, we may be inclined to forget it, but no matter how much we insist on the language diversity in America or the value of foreign languages, we must not forget the great national advantage we have in the dominance of English. There is no place in Europe and not many places in the world where there is such a great expanse of so many people speaking the same language in a relatively uniform way. The uniformity of American English, compared to the regional dialects in England, already existed in the eighteenth century. Observers pointed out that there had been dialect leveling in the United States so that the regional differences were not nearly as great; there were regional varieties of a more or less standard kind of English, instead of the deep morphological and phonological differences of local British dialects.

However, when I say 'relative uniformity' and point to the advantage of all being able to communicate with one another over a great area, I am not saying that there are no variations in the language. One of the most fascinating things about American English is its regional, social, and registral variation. Strangely enough, in spite of all the work on American dialects, we still have no adequate measure of the variation, and we have no baseline against which to measure changes in English diversity over time in America. For example, if someone claims that the great use of television has led to increased uniformity in American English and our regional dialects are dying out, there is no way we can easily check this. If someone claims that because of certain social issues in our cities, the social dialect variation in urban centers is increasing and there are more differences in the English of various social classes, occupations, and ethnic groups than there used to be in American English, there is no way we can check that either. You would think that at some time in the course of our history we would have made a baseline study with samples of English from various parts of the country, various social classes, and various uses of languages, such as in the classroom, the press, or the pulpit. If we had done so, we could measure ourselves every ten years or so and have some factual basis for estimates of the way diversity is changing in English.

Well, what other languages are there here besides American English? First we must notice the indigenous languages, those that really belong here, those that were here first. I am talking about the Native American languages. We tend to forget that there are at least 50 or so American Indian languages still spoken here. Many of them are viable languages for their communities. The monolingual speakers of Indian languages are getting fewer, but in many cases, American Indian languages are being kept as home languages and languages of group identification. We might notice also that in the last few years there has been a renewed interest in the use of American Indian languages and a recognition of their value. This is so partly because of their structural diversity and value to linguistics for understanding the nature of human language, but, more importantly, for communicative purposes in American life.

I think we would next notice what Fishman has referred to as our 'colonial languages', the languages that came over here in the very early days, before there was a republic. I am thinking, in particular, of Spanish, but there are other languages that fit in that category as well. In many parts of the United States, Spanish was present before English appeared, and Spanish plays a special role in the United States; in terms of number of speakers, it is clearly the most important language after English.

Next we would notice the 'immigrant languages', generally the languages of people who came here expecting to lose their language, either wanting to become Americanized and thus getting rid of their language, or wanting to come to America for other reasons, but recognizing that they sooner or later were likely to lose their language. I think, for example, of Italian, which was mentioned last night by Congressman Panetta. Speakers of Italian, after those who speak Spanish and probably German, constitute the largest speech community in this country although they do not have nearly the visibility and the general recognition that speakers of other languages do. Last night someone used the expression, 'coming out of the closet' about the use of other languages (whether it was Congressman Panetta talking about Italian or Jim Alatis talking about Greek, I do not remember). Whoever said it was referring to a new phenomenon: whereas just a generation ago--in fact half a generation ago--we did not like to admit to our immigrant languages, now people are searching for them and are beginning to see how important they are for their own ethnic heritage and community life. But, whether we are ignoring or fostering our immigrant languages, the fact is that America is still a multilingual country. There are many languages spoken by thousands and in some cases by over a million speakers; these languages have played important roles in America and will continue to do so. I should be able to make a list of the top ones; I am not sure I could get the right order but I suspect that, after Spanish, it is something like: German, Italian, Polish, Yiddish, and if we could only lump all of the Scandinavian languages together as one language, that one would belong pretty high on the list too.

When we debate the pros and cons of bilingual education today, we tend to forget that this issue has been debated before in the history of America and that bilingual education flourished in a number of cities for many decades. For example, German was used in bilingual education in both parochial schools and public schools in such cities as Cleveland and St. Louis. This issue is one that we have known in the past and is back with us again.

Before I get to the question I want to ask concerning the language situation in the United States, I would like to note the pattern that foreign language teaching in our schools and colleges has had. We all bewail the decline in foreign language teaching, and I bewail it as much as anyone here, I am sure, but if we look at which languages are taught and why, a strange pattern emerges. French, German, Spanish, and Latin are the basic foreign languages in American education and, setting Latin aside, it is difficult to see what justification there is for the three particular modern languages in the pattern. We can understand how they came on the scene: English, French, and German were the three international languages in Europe, and there was a time when French and German scholarship was necessary for American researchers. For example, if you were in organic chemistry, you had to read all the books in German, and if you were interested in international diplomacy you had to read the articles in French. This is no longer true in the same way. For scientific literature, English is by far the most important vehicle, Russian is second, and many other languages are used in scholarly publications around the world. So scholarly research can no longer be the reason. If we think of the study of great literatures--and there are great literatures in those languages to be sure--there are also great literatures in many other languages of Europe and for that matter, of Asia and other parts of the world. If we think the pattern has to do with our ethnic heritages, the immigrant languages in the United States, we have to ask why Italian and Polish are not there. Apparently, the selection policy was never thought through. Perhaps this policy is the right one for foreign language teaching in the United States. I am not saying the decision is wrong--but the traditional pattern just grew without careful investigation or planning. Now as we talk about reviving the teaching of foreign languages, as we talk about getting some kind of language requirements back into our universities, improving the teaching of languages, and teaching certain levels of proficiency, we might also examine just which languages should be taught and what levels of proficiency are needed for what purposes.

Having taken a look at the language situation in the world and the language situation in the United States, we now come to the question I want to ask. What is our American language policy? That is, what is our response as a people and as a nation to the national and international needs and resources in the use of language or, to use the words of this conference, where should language fit in American life? It is possible that we have no overall policy. If that is so, should we be working toward one? It is also possible that we do have an implicit unarticulated policy about language, and if so, shouldn't we find out what it is, make it explicit, and examine it? I was very much interested in some of the comments along this line made by the speakers last night, and I am looking forward with interest to comments to be made on that topic today.

In putting this question, I do not mean to suggest that I think we should have a national policy which would set legal controls on the use of language in America. Nothing could be further from the American way of governing ourselves. Nothing could be further from my own feelings on this subject. We must keep our freedom of choice as individuals and as communities, as institutions, and as local units of education and government. But in putting the question, I am revealing my own conviction that the time is ripe, and perhaps long overdue, for some Americans--including some of our national leaders and the Federal Commission on International Studies and Foreign Languages, if it comes into being--to devote thought and effort to the formulation of a national language policy or set of policies which could move us toward the conservation of our present language resources and the strengthening of our resources where necessary, to meet the foreseeable language needs of our nation, for its internal strength and for its proper role in the family of nations.

Such a policy would, for example, strengthen our language resources in American English. It might do so by fostering research on the rich variety of our principal language, by more effective teaching of basic skills of language use for the varied needs of our society, and by the recognition of a broader range of uses of English than many of our current curricula embody.

Such a policy would give appropriate place to our minority languages, whether indigenous languages, colonial languages, or immigrant languages, not only by the provision of bilingual education where this is effective, but also in the provision for excellence at advanced levels of language use in higher education, in mass media, and so on, to the extent that particular language communities are willing to work for this, and to the extent that it is socially and economically feasible for the nation as a whole.

Such a policy would examine the need for foreign language teaching at various levels in our educational systems and the value of language study, for its profound effect in the growth and development of individuals, its role in the world of business and the professions, and its indispensable contribution to communication between the United

States and the rest of the world. Decisions on which foreign languages to teach, at which levels, and for what purposes, could be determined not only by the natural forces of our own educational history, but also by the rational consideration of resources and needs. Our policy on foreign language teaching could build on the growing body of language-acquisition research in America. America is the world's leader in quality research in first and second language acquisition, but it is probably the world's poorest consumer of that research.

Once, some years ago, I was giving a lecture in Sweden on applied linguistics, in particular, second language teaching. It was a graduate seminar and the students were very much interested; they had all kinds of good questions and we had a really fine discussion. Everybody seemed happy with our session when suddenly it occurred to me: Here I am speaking English to this group of Swedish graduate students, and if I had come there and spoken French or German, that whole seminar could have gone just as well. But I could not think of a single university in America where you could have had a graduate seminar on second language research at which a visiting lecturer could have addressed the group in another language and where the group could have followed the lecture and used the lecturer's language freely. I had the strange feeling come over me: what am I doing here telling Swedes how to learn languages or teach them? And, yet, the fact remains that the kind of research that I was reporting on was of great interest to them; some of those present were interested in how such research could be applied in their educational system.

Finally, a national language policy would acknowledge the special place of English in the language situation of the world and in the language situation of our own country, and would prepare us to assume our natural position of leadership, in full cooperation with other English-speaking nations, in the further spreading of English as a world language, without, however, tying it directly to our own political and cultural values.

Of course, these particular points and the examples chosen reflect my own biases and predilections. I could doubtless be educated out of some of them and could be convinced that others are more important, but the basic question remains: What is our language policy? And my basic conviction remains: it is time we devoted more effort to the development of a national response to the language resources and needs at home and abroad.

LANGUAGE AND COGNITION: DIRECTIONS AND IMPLICATIONS

WILGA M. RIVERS
Harvard University

Cognition is a term which is vaguely understood. It is like ecology: accepted in general as 'a good thing', often without a very clear idea of its implications or applications. If we take from the scholarly journal Cognition what a group of serious scholars of cognition consider to be their area of concern, we come up with 'the study of the mind'. 'Contributions from the fields of psychology, linguistics, neurophysiology, ethology, philosophy, and epistemology', we read, 'can find a place in this journal, provided that they have some bearing on the functioning of the mind' (Cognition 1.1, 1972).

Interest in the functioning of the mind, that is, in cognitive processes, has a long history. Nor has it been ignored in the comparatively short life of the science of psychology. Miller (1962) and Blumenthal (1970) recount for us in detail the intense activity in this area in the later part of the nineteenth century: research associated particularly with the names of Wundt, Bühler, and James; and Bartlett's book on Remembering, published in 1932, has much to say that is of interest to contemporary researchers. These psychologists of an earlier period realized the fundamental role of the phenomenon of human language in unlocking many of the mysteries of mental life.

A similar position was taken by Chomsky, who, in the sixties, reminded linguists and psychologists that 'the study of language may very well, as was traditionally supposed, provide a remarkably favorable perspective for the study of human mental processes' (Chomsky 1968:84).

Particularly in the case of language it is natural to expect a close relation between innate properties of the mind and

32

features of linguistic structure; for language, after all, has
no existence apart from its mental representation. Whatever
properties it has must be those that are given to it by the
innate mental processes of the organism that has invented it
and that invents it anew with each succeeding generation,
along with whatever properties are associated with the conditions of its use (Chomsky 1968:81).

In what sense language may be considered innate is a matter of
research and controversy. (Chomsky is, of course, referring to
abstract representations of fundamental linguistic relations.) It is,
however, a matter of common observation, as well as documented
research (Lenneberg 1967:125-141), that with rare exceptions human
infants with some contact with language-using human beings acquire
an exceedingly complex linguistic system at an age when abstract
reasoning is normally not in evidence. Whether innate properties of
the mind directly determine linguistic structure or whether these
same properties determine human behavior in ways which make the
universality of certain basic features of human language inevitable
in the general conditions of human existence is yet to be determined.
   G. Lakoff (1972:77) asserts that 'the linguistic elements used in
grammar have an independent natural basis in the human conceptual
system'. Stated in this form, the innate nature of language is more
compatible with the position of a psychologist (or psycholinguist)
like Bever. Bever deplores the artificial separation of 'knowledge'
of a language (competence) from actual language use (performance),
a distinction popularized by Chomsky, and raises the question
'whether the acquisition of language systems is best interpreted in
terms of the primary acquisition of a series of grammatically defined
rules or in terms of the development of the psychological systems
underlying perception and memory' (Bever 1970:341). Once the
structural and behavioral systems of language are viewed as 'special
expressions of cognitive universals', which are already the subject
of intense research, the cognitive psychologist with a particular
interest in language can turn his attention to solving the basic problem:
'how the different innate components [of language acquisition] are
linked together in the course of language learning and how the learned
aspects are incorporated in adult language behavior' (Bever 1970:341).
   Bruner (1974/75) and Halliday (1973) take another approach to the
presumably innate aspects of language. They seek to identify the
communicative needs of infants as revealed in their prelinguistic and
early linguistic behavior. In this behavior they find early indications
of the functions of language in use in speech acts (see Rivers 1976b).
'Use', as Bruner has observed (1974/75:283), 'is a powerful deter-
minant of rule structure'. To Bruner, language acquisition takes

place in a joint 'action dialogue' between infant and adult (1974/75: 284).

Bruner points out that even an innate Language Acquisition Device, as proposed by Chomsky (1965:30-34), would require a program to guide it in the recognition of which of the humanly possible languages it was encountering. It is the nature of this program that interests cognitive psychologists. (This is another way of restating the problem Bever posed.) Bruner prefers to turn his attention to the role played in the development of syntactic competence by the uses to which language is put in different contexts. 'Initial language at least', he says (1974/75:261) 'has a pragmatic base structure'. As infants grow in experience in social interaction, they gain insight into linguistic ways of expressing ideas they previously held by other than linguistic means; in other words, they learn 'who is doing what with what object toward whom in whose possession and in what location and often by what instrumentality' (Bruner 1974/75:271).

Semantically based relations such as these, which derive from the work of Fillmore (1968) and Chafe (1970), have been found useful in the study of child language by researchers other than Bruner. Brown (1973) and Schlesinger (1977) have also found them more descriptive of what the child is acquiring than the syntactic relations basic to the now classical form of transformational-generative grammar. Once the notion that the child's first linguistic task is the acquisition of an abstract system of syntactic relations is rejected in favor of an acquisition based on the functions of language in use, the theoretical assumptions are more easily aligned with the stages of cognitive development from infancy to maturity postulated by Piaget (1958) and with his emphasis on the operative aspect of the symbol (Furth 1969:99-105). Giving orders, asking for things, stating who does what to whom, and expressing needs and wishes are all possible at the stage when language is being acquired, whereas ability to recognize and express abstract relations comes nearer puberty.

It is interesting to observe in this one area of cognitive studies the shift of emphasis in less than 20 years from syntax, to study of human conceptual and perceptual systems, to a pragmatic approach to language in situations of use. In the present state of research we can in no way claim that there is a direct parallel between first and second language learning, particularly in the case of the acquisition of a new language by adolescents and adults in the formal situations in which so many people do such learning. These are the types of situations to which Subsection D of Part 4 of the Helsinki Agreement ('Foreign Languages and Civilizations') addresses itself, with its emphasis on secondary education, higher education, and adult education (ADFL 1977:46).

Whether similar processes are involved in first- and second-
language acquisition is probably the most ancient and vigorous controversy in the whole area of language-related studies, although it is
frequently discussed on the basis of anecdotal, rather than experimental, evidence. The apparent insolubility of this controversy can,
to some extent, be traced to the differing levels of generality at which
the various disputants are developing their arguments. Do they mean,
for instance, that adolescent/adult students of English learn the uses
of the definite and indefinite articles in English in exactly the same
way, making the same errors along the way, as do children growing
up in English-speaking families? Or, on the other hand, are they
maintaining that adolescent/adult students learn to use a new language
through practice in its use in the normal functions of communication,
as do young children, rather than through detailed explanation of the
rule system? That the development of precise structures runs
parallel has yet to be conclusively demonstrated, while the second
position is overly simplified and dichotomous. To some extent a
further extension of the old educational adage, 'we learn what we do',
it ignores the varying linguistic abilities and experiences, the learning preferences, and the individual motives and goals of mature students in widely diverse circumstances. Unfortunately, the 'language-
learning situation' at all levels and in all circumstances cannot be
simplified and unified to this degree, as all experienced teachers are
aware.

Nevertheless, research in first-language acquisition has had a
very strong influence on the fledgling field of second-language acquisition, which, with notable exceptions, has in the main turned its attention to the acquisition of a second language by young children in informal settings or bilingual classes. (The study of children growing
up in a bilingual environment has a somewhat longer history dating
back, according to Leopold, at least to Ronjat in 1913 (see Leopold
in Bar-Adon and Leopold, eds., 1971:12). As the second-language
acquisition field matures, we may hope that there will be more studies
of adolescent/adult second-language learners in formal instructional
situations, like that of Schachter 1974, to provide a useful complement, if not corrective, to the general preoccupations of this research.

The earliest second-language acquisition studies of the recent cycle
focused to a great extent on the plausibility of the notion of transfer,
particularly negative transfer or interference, from what was learned
in the first language. This was to some extent a reaction to the overly
optimistic emphasis on transfer in the preceding decades that had led
to, or paralleled, a plethora of studies which contrasted features of
pairs of languages and, in some cases, attempted to predict problem
areas for the learners of these languages. Without wishing to cover
the ground already comprehensively covered in the very thorough

evaluative review of 'Trends in second-language acquisition research' by Hakuta and Cancino (1977), I shall make here certain personal observations on the directions and implications of this aspect of cognitive research and indicate where I feel it may find more fruitful territory.

Controversy has raged on whether errors made by second-language learners represent negative transfer (interference) from first-language habits of use or are really developmental errors of a universal character, since they are often similar to those made by first-language learners at a similar stage in their control of a language (Dulay and Burt 1975:24-25). Even errors which seem to provide clear evidence of the use of first-language grammatical rules in the second language have been taken by some writers to be the result of the active process of testing the hypothesis that the second language operates on similar principles to the first language, rather than as the transfer of first-language habits (Corder 1967). This parallels the theoretical position (derived from Chomsky 1965:30), that first-language learners are testing hypotheses as to the nature of the language they are learning. Since Corder's hypothesis-testing assumption is providing a different explanation of the same observable phenomenon which others call transfer, his thesis can be validated only as one segment of a complete theoretical orientation.

It may be observed at this point that when one is testing a hypothesis, a serious disconfirmation makes one seek immediately another hypothesis which seems to fit the facts. In using the foreign language one is learning, however, one often continues to make the same error, even when one knows the languages operate differently for expressing this particular meaning. The notion that one is testing the hypothesis that the two languages operate in a parallel fashion in these cases is difficult to sustain in light of the fact (frequently observed and experienced) that one is constantly repeating the same error and then immediately correcting oneself, often with a sense of mortification and exasperation at one's inability to perform according to rules one has been taught and feels one 'knows'.

In quantitative calculations of errors in studies based on the developmental and hypothesis-testing assumptions, no estimate seems to have been made of the amount of positive transfer from first-language learning at those points where the rule systems run parallel. This is no doubt much more difficult to demonstrate than it is to distinguish errors genuinely due to negative transfer. Without including positive as well as negative transfer in the assessment, however, any conclusions about the amount of transfer, which are based on the data, rest moot. Again, as in our earlier discussion, we may query here the level at which evidence of 'interference' or transfer (which is the preferable term) is sought by the investigators.

The investigator may be looking for evidence of interference at the morphological level, as some have done. Let us consider the situation of an English speaker learning a Romance language. In the subject's first language, in this case English, the third person singular of the present tense of most verbs takes an ending which is not used for the other persons for which an unmarked form, resembling the radical of the verb, is used. In the second language, the student does not attempt to add an ending to the third person of the verb while continuing to use only the radical for the other persons. As a result, it may be asserted by some that there is no evidence of interference from first-language habits of use. The discussion may, however, be conducted at a higher level of conceptualization. The subject, we may say, is unaccustomed to using marked forms of the verb for person, number, and tense in the first language, except in one or two very frequent positions which have been learned through constant use as exceptions to the general rule; he therefore finds it difficult to develop an awareness of the necessity to attach a variety of endings to verb stems to make these distinctions. As a result, when trying to communicate, this subject tends to use radicals in most situations, these being the closest approximation to the unmarked forms which he is accustomed to use in his first language. (This tendency is regarded in many current studies as simplification of the type used by children learning their first language.)

To take a further example, another second-language learner may have developed, while learning the first language, the concept that gender makes a clear semantic distinction, with rare exceptions, as in English. When this learner finds that grammatical gender distinctions, apparently unmotivated, pervade the second language, she may find it hard to conceive of these distinctions as important enough to affect practically every part of speech--nouns, adjectives, articles, pronouns, and even some forms of the verb. Although this has been explained to her, she still has to make a conscious mental effort to keep this all-pervading concept in mind when applying lower-level rules of agreement in all kinds of positions and relationships. The particular errors she makes may be interpreted as intralingual, as simplification or as overgeneralization errors, whereas the basic problem is an interlingual conceptual contrast. (For terminology, see Selinker 1972.) To my mind, much more attention should be paid in classroom teaching to the comprehension and thorough assimilation of these fundamental conceptual differences between languages, so that students are learning to operate within the total language system, rather than picking up minor skills in its application. In the same vein, it is essential that the student acquire an understanding of the different way a new language sees and expresses temporal relationships across the language system, rather than concentrating

exclusively on particular uses of particular tenses and the correct
forms for these uses (see Rivers 1968). Without a conceptual grasp
of such overriding interlingual contrasts, the second-language learner
will be unable to use effectively the lower-level knowledge of para-
digms and rules which have strictly limited application.

A similar psychological problem is demonstrated in the common
phenomenon of English-speaking students of French who find it hard
to comprehend what the use of the subjunctive rather than the indicative conveys to a native speaker of French. They have never inter-
nalized the overriding concept that the use of the subjunctive mood conveys a subjective view of the situation (that is, a personal opinion) as
opposed to the objective view of the indicative. Thus, je ne pense pas
qu'il soit parti implies that I am not giving factual information, but my
own assessment of the situation, whereas je pense qu'il est déjà parti
is based on some objective clues and may well be followed by an explanation like parce que la porte de son bureau est fermée. Because
they lack such a higher level concept, English-speaking students of
French tend to spatter subjunctive forms everywhere in the hope that
some will stick in the right places. This insecurity and uncertainty
about the extent of applicability of new rules, because of a lack of
knowledge of how they fit into the language system, is a distinctly
different psychological phenomenon from that of overgeneralization,
which is described by Selinker (1972:218) as the extension of a newly
acquired second-language rule 'to an environment in which, to the
learner, it could logically apply, but just does not'. (Selinker would
categorize as overgeneralization the extension of the use of the past
tense morpheme of walk/walked to go/goed: an error commonly made
by English-speaking children, even though they may previously have
known and used went.) Psychologically, the phenomenon I am dis-
cussing seems to share some of the features of the native-language
phenomenon of hypercorrection and may perhaps be better described
as overcompensation: an attitude of better more than less.

Experimentation conducted at this level of conceptualization,
rather than at the level of the morpheme, might produce more interesting insights into the problems of adolescent/adult second-language
learners. Whether one is referring here to habits of thought and
approach to language use developed through using the first language,
or to hypotheses the second-language learner is making about the new
language, is difficult to say. Perhaps we should ask them, as is done
in some other psychological experiments with mature subjects (see
Schachter, Tyson, and Diffley 1976). Until errors can be identified
as interlingual (due to transfer from the first to the second language)
or intralingual (deriving from elements within the second language
itself) by some more clearly demonstrable psychological criteria,
interpretation of research in this area will remain somewhat hazy.

Once we can clarify what we are dealing with, we may find, as Hakuta and Cancino maintain (1977:299), that 'interference errors in second-language learning are fine examples of language transfer and . . . strongly point to areas of dynamic interplay between the two languages'.

Evidence that the adolescent/adult learner is very conscious of the points where the rule system of the second language diverges from that of the first language is provided by avoidance studies like those of Schachter (1974). In an interesting investigation using written compositions in English, she found that while it appeared in quantitative data that a group with a contrasting relative pronoun rule system in their first language made fewer errors than a group whose first-language relative pronoun rule system was similar to that of English, another approach to the data revealed that the first group were avoiding the use of rules to which they were not accustomed and which they therefore found difficult. Ipso facto, fewer uses of relative pronouns by the subjects yielded fewer errors in their use. Schachter concluded that if students find particular constructions in the target language difficult to comprehend, it is very likely that they will try to avoid producing them (Schachter 1974:213).

Clearly, much more needs to be done on what may be considered transfer from first-language learning and use to second-language learning and use.

It is interesting to note that, as with first-language acquisition studies, second-language acquisition research has been moving from an almost single-minded emphasis on the acquisition of the syntactic and morphological rules of the second language to strategies of language in use to meet the needs of communication. It is here that we can place Hakuta's prefabricated utterances, which are learned as units to be plugged into speech acts (Hakuta and Cancino 1977:309-310), and Hatch's discourse analysis (Hatch 1977) which examines, in second-language situations, communicative exchanges which recall the joint 'action dialogue' of Bruner's studies and what Brown calls 'episodes'.

It must be emphasized that studies with very young children in bilingual situations do not produce particularly relevant insights into the strategies employed by linguistically and conceptually mature adolescent/adult learners (see Rivers 1977). The input of the latter is determined by their textbooks and other learning materials and they have well-established patterns of interaction from much experience in communication in their first language. Research into strategies of language use within the corpus with which the student has become acquainted at a particular stage of classroom learning would be very interesting and enlightening for hard-pressed classroom teachers. A full-time teacher carrying the typical school

teaching load and teaching the usual large group is far too busy inter-
acting with many students during class hours to study the linguistic
and pragmatic reactions of individuals analytically. What I am proposing here is not the study of the 'interlanguage' of particular students at specific points in their acquisition of the foreign language
(although this can be enlightening). I am referring rather to strategies foreign-language learner-users employ to make 'infinite use of
finite means' (Chomsky 1965:8, quoting Humboldt). When these
strategies have been identified and described, they may be encouraged or even taught and incorporated into teaching materials.

From the discussion to this point it would seem that cognitive
studies of interest to teachers of a new language are to be found only
in the area of first- and second-language acquisition. Such an
assumption would be most misleading. Cognitive studies cover such
vast areas that, at this point, I can merely indicate other ongoing
research which should provide exciting new insights. I have dealt
with the implications of some of this work elsewhere (Rivers 1971,
1972, 1975, 1977; Melvin and Rivers 1976; and Rivers and Melvin
1977).

As teachers of second or foreign languages we are interested in
how human beings perceive messages (in speech or writing) and how
they process and interpret them (Neisser 1967). We are interested
in the way new information is transformed by receivers as they relate
it to information already stored; how what they receive is recorded
and organized for storage, not as atomic items but within complex
semantic networks; how recoded information moves from short-term
to long-term storage and how it is retrieved, often with the greatest
of ease after long periods, at other times after a concentrated mental
search (Tulving and Donaldson 1972). Even if memory should prove
to have a chemical base in the RNA, we still need to know how memory
processes work. We gain new insights from studies of semantic and
episodic memory (Klatzky 1975) and the latter encourages us to
teach language in situational contexts of some reality. Melvin (1976)
has drawn interesting implications from artificial intelligence (computer simulation) experiments and information processing (IP) theory.

We are interested in forgetting, which is intricately involved with
the concept of memory as an active process, not as a repository of
inert items. This leads us to what will be remembered. Here we
are at one of the interfaces between cognitive and dynamic psychology,
because what we process from what we perceive is related to individual motivation and meaningfulness. (Even the question of what is
meaningful for the learner is far from being a simple issue.) We can
learn much also from studies of concept development, particularly
crosscultural conceptualization and, for the teaching of another

culture, we need to understand the formation and retention of stereo-
types and how these may be adapted and changed.

Further, we need to know how human beings select messages to
achieve their purposes and then compose utterances to convey these
messages to others, and we must view these processes from the pragmatic as well as the syntactic and phonological points of view. Finally,
I have not even touched on the intense study of the last few years in the
areas of cerebral dominance and the aphasias (Lenneberg and Lenneberg 1975).

This rapid survey demonstrates dramatically the importance of
cognitive studies for those of us who teach languages, yet far too little
is known about them by language teachers, program designers, and
materials writers. Certainly cognition is a burgeoning field and much
has been but sketchily researched at present; positions are taken and
abandoned somewhat rapidly as experimental data are reexamined and
reinterpreted. Yesterday's dogma may be a devalued currency before
it can receive serious applied consideration. Yet much that is fundamental is retained and recombined in the evolution of theory. As
Neisser has expressed it (1967:4-5): 'the cognitive theorist . . .
cannot make assumptions casually, for they must conform to the results of 100 years of experimentation'.

Cognition is a field we cannot and must not ignore. It is from
solid research in this area that we may hope to develop criteria by
which to evaluate the appropriateness and potential effectiveness of
the many techniques of language teaching which seem to rise and
recede like the tide at regular intervals--serving their purpose of
refreshing the scene, but often carrying away with them indiscrimi-
nately both useful and dispensable practices.

If we wish to improve and expand the teaching of second and third
languages in this country, providing everyone who seeks such knowledge with the most effective learning situation we can devise, we
must not only support research in areas of cognition, but study its
results, and incorporate them into the training of our teachers and
the preparation of materials. As in every other field of endeavor,
nothing comes without effort and helping another person to acquire
another language will never be easy.

REFERENCES

Bartlett, F. C. 1932. Remembering. Cambridge: At the University
    Press.
Bever, T. G. 1970. The cognitive basis for linguistic structures.
    In: Cognition and the development of language. Edited by J. R.
    Hayes. New York and London: John Wiley and Sons.

Blumenthal, A. L. 1970. Language and psychology. Historical aspects of psycholinguistics. New York and London: John Wiley and Sons.

Brown, R. 1973. A first language. The early stages. Cambridge, Massachusetts: Harvard University Press.

Bruner, J. S. 1974/75. From communication to language--A psychological perspective. Cognition 3(3). 255-87.

Chafe, W. L. 1970. Meaning and the structure of language. Chicago: The University of Chicago Press.

Chomsky, N. 1965. Aspects of the theory of syntax. Cambridge, Massachusetts: The MIT Press.

Chomsky, N. 1968. Language and mind. New York: Harcourt, Brace and World.

Corder, S. P. 1967. The significance of learners' errors. IRAL 5. 161-70.

Dulay, H. C., and M. K. Burt. 1975. Creative construction in second language learning and teaching. In: New directions in second language learning, teaching, and bilingual education. Edited by M. K. Burt and H. C. Dulay. Washington, D. C.: Teachers of English to Speakers of Other Languages (TESOL).

Fillmore, C. J. 1968. The case for case. In: Universals of linguistic theory. Edited by E. Bach and R. T. Harms. New York: Holt, Rinehart and Winston.

Furth, H. G. 1969. Piaget and knowledge. Theoretical foundations. Englewood Cliffs, N. J.: Prentice-Hall, Inc.

Halliday, M. A. K. 1973. Explorations in the functions of language. London: Edward Arnold.

Hakuta, K., and H. Cancino. 1977. Trends in second-language acquisition research. Harvard Educational Review 47(3). 294-316.

Hatch, E., ed. 1977. Studies in second language acquisition. A book of readings. Rowley, Massachusetts: Newbury House Publishers.

Inhelder, B., and J. Piaget. 1958. The growth of logical thinking from childhood to adolescence. Translated by A. Parsons and S. Milgram. New York: Basic Books.

Klatzky, R. L. 1975. Human memory: Structures and processes. San Francisco: W. H. Freeman.

Lakoff, G. 1972. The arbitrary basis of transformational grammar. Lg. 48. 76-87.

Lenneberg, E. H. 1967. Biological foundations of language. New York and London: John Wiley and Sons.

Lenneberg, E. H., and E. Lenneberg. 1975. Foundations of language development. A multidisciplinary approach. Vols. 1 and 2. New York and London: Academic Press, and Paris: The UNESCO Press.

Leopold, W. F. 1948. The study of child language and infant bilingualism. Reprinted in: Child language. A book of readings. Edited by A. Bar-Adon and W. F. Leopold. Englewood Cliffs, N. J.: Prentice-Hall, 1971.

Melvin, B. S. 1976. Recent research in memory and cognition and its implications for second-language teaching. Unpublished Ph. D. dissertation. University of Illinois at Urbana-Champaign.

Melvin, B. S., and W. M. Rivers. 1976. In one ear and out the other: Implications of memory studies for comprehension and production. In: On TESOL, 1976. Edited by J. Fanselow and R. Crymes. Washington, D. C.: TESOL.

Miller, G. A. 1964. Psychology. The science of mental life. London: Hutchinson and Co.

Neisser, U. 1967. Cognitive psychology. New York: Appleton-Century-Crofts.

Rivers, W. M. 1968. Contrastive linguistics in textbook and classroom. Reprinted in: Rivers 1976a.

Rivers, W. M. 1971. Linguistic and psychological factors in speech perception and their implications for teaching materials. Reprinted in: Rivers 1976a.

Rivers, W. M. 1972. The foreign-language teacher and cognitive psychology or where do we go from here? Reprinted in: Rivers 1976a.

Rivers, W. M. 1975. A practical guide to the teaching of French. New York and London: Oxford University Press.

Rivers, W. M. 1976a. Speaking in many tongues. Essays in foreign-language teaching. Expanded 2d ed. Rowley, Massachusetts: Newbury House Publishers.

Rivers, W. M. 1976b. The natural and the normal in language learning. In: Papers in second language acquisition. Edited by H. D. Brown. Language Learning, special issue No. 4.

Rivers, W. M. 1977. Language learning and language teaching--any relationship? In: Principles of second language learning and teaching. Edited by W. C. Ritchie. New York and London: Academic Press.

Rivers, W. M., and B. S. Melvin. 1977. Memory and memorization in comprehension and production: Contributions of IP theory. Canadian Modern Language Review 33.497-502.

Schachter, J. 1974. An error in error analysis. Language Learning 24.205-214.

Schachter, J., A. F. Tyson, and F. J. Diffley. 1976. Learner intuitions of grammaticality. Language Learning 26.67-76.

Schlesinger, I. M. 1977. Production and comprehension of utterances. Hillsdale, N. J.: Lawrence Erlbaum Associates.

Selinker, L. 1972. Interlanguage. IRAL 10.219-231.

The Helsinki Agreement and foreign languages. ADFL Bulletin, Vol. 8, No. 3 (March, 1977):46.

Tulving, E., and W. Donaldson. 1972. Organization of memory. New York and London: Academic Press.

THE ROLE OF ENGLISH IN
GLOBAL INTERDEPENDENCE

HAROLD B. ALLEN
University of Minnesota

In the spring of 1959 I was showing to the British-trained English
teachers in the Nokrashi preparatory school in Cairo some placards
with line drawings of American scenes. Among them was the interior
of a drugstore, with the familiar soda fountain. One teacher peered
at a sign over the fountain and then, with obvious surprise, asked me,
'Do you have Coca-Cola in the United States, too?' Inevitably, we
then had a discussion of the role of culture in teaching English as a
foreign language.

That role is an important one and the title of this paper would
allow its consideration here, but I am asking you instead to attend
to the teaching of English itself as a component of foreign policy.
Life is sometimes said to be a matter of ups and downs. You will
now hear first about the up and then about the down in the life of English as a foreign language in the context of our international relations.

First, the 'up'.

Just as the teaching of English followed the spread of British
dominion in the Empire and then in the Commonwealth, so it developed in the expansion of American interests after World War II.
The growing governmental awareness of the role of the English language in these interests appeared with different emphases in various
government agencies--sometimes cultural, sometimes political,
sometimes economic. Because no omniscient prophet had foreseen
this development, no single overall plan guided those who sought to
meet on an ad hoc basis the needs they encountered. The resulting
duplication and overlapping of overseas efforts led the then Assistant
Secretary of State for Educational and Cultural Affairs to create, in
1959, an interagency working group, later to be known as the

Interagency Committee on English Language Teaching. Its primary functions were informational, with respect to agency plans and the value of coordinating efforts in the foreign field and agency participation in conferences on English teaching. But such coordination appeared to have so little effect abroad that two years later an ad hoc conference sponsored in Washington by the International Cooperation Administration and the Center for Applied Linguistics recommended the appointment of a small permanent nongovernmental group to promote the desired interchange of information and also to provide the government agencies with professional assistance from academic specialists. This group, the National Advisory Council on Teaching English as a Foreign Language (NACTEFL) met first in 1962 and afterward semiannually or annually until 1975. At its meetings it received reports from the several agencies and prepared for them constructive professional decisions reflecting the Council's reactions.

What agencies have been reporting to NACTEFL concerning our English teaching activities in other countries? They are the State Department's Cultural Affairs Division (CU), the Agency for International Development (AID), the United States Information Agency (USIA), the Office of Education, the Peace Corps, and the Department of Defense. Their varied activities roughly parallel those which in England are the function of a single semiautonomous agency, the British Council. For a number of years the Council's multiple American counterparts bore America's share of our mutual responsibility, the teaching of English as a foreign language. Their impressive activity began slowly with involvement in Latin America in 1939. It peaked about 1970, when the onset of a serious downslide reversed the trend.

Although American overseas efforts lacked the administrative focus provided in the British Council, repeated policy statements sought to offer such a focus. In 1961 the Center for Applied Linguistics ad hoc conference agreed that the teaching of English is of such critical international significance as to call for a sustained national emphasis. Hence it was imperative, the conference concluded, that the government take the necessary steps to formulate long-range strategy and policy. One year later, in 1962, Philip Coombs, then the Assistant Secretary of State for Educational Policy and Cultural Affairs, responded by telling the participants in the first meeting of NACTEFL that the problem of 'English as a foreign language is crucial and hence has priority in the government'. Because of the tremendous motivation for learning English, he said--from that of the elevator operator in the Istanbul Hilton to that of the school club in Africa seeking to use library books and listen to the radio--'a massive effort is required of the United States'.

Coombs's successor, Lucius Battle, said at the second meeting of NACTEFL in 1963 that Secretary Dean Rusk was spearheading a new awareness of the important role of the English language in United States foreign policy with respect to both economic and cultural implications. He indicated the need for coordination and unity with his example of seventeen different American governmental and private agencies engaged in teaching English in Ankara, Turkey.

Most important of all such policy statements was that signed by President Lyndon B. Johnson on June 11, 1965, as enunciating the official United States position. It read, in part, as follows:

The rapidly growing interest in English cuts across ideological lines . . . Demands for learning English are widespread. The United States ought to respond to these demands. English is a key which opens doors to scientific and technical knowledge indispensable to the economic and political development of vast areas of the world. An increase in the knowledge of English can contribute directly to greater understanding among nations . . . The United States government is prepared, as a major policy, to be of active and friendly assistance to countries that desire such help in the teaching and utilization of English.

How did the achievements match these statements of need and policy? They are so many and so varied that I can only sample and generalize, in the hope that this may be sufficient to provide at least an awareness of what thousands of dedicated English teachers and consultants, through government support, have been able to contribute since 1965.

Department of State. State's Division of Educational Policy and Cultural Affairs (CU) has sponsored many programs to strengthen patterns of informal communication in order to influence the environment in which our foreign policy is carried out and to enlarge the circle of those able to serve as influential interpreters between the United States and other nations.

Beginning in 1939, State steadily expanded in Latin America a program for sending American professors to Latin American universities, bringing teachers and administrators here for development programs in English, sending United States specialists to teach seminars for secondary school teachers of English, and developing English orientation programs for students heading for graduate work in American universities. These programs were particularly successful in Brazil, Colombia, Ecuador, and Mexico.

In the 1950s the program expanded greatly. Teachers and exchanges, sometimes with summer seminars, were provided for Japan, Thailand, Indonesia, Vietnam, Iran, Turkey, Greece, Italy, Spain, Portugal, Lebanon, the USSR, Poland, Romania, Yugoslavia, Czechoslovakia, Egypt, Syria, and several African countries. Recent specific actions are the 1970 agreement that sends 25 American TESL teachers to Spanish teacher-training institutes and brings 27 Spanish secondary school teachers of English here for a year of advanced training; the 1973 arrangement with Hungary that has brought three graduate students to the University of Minnesota to obtain the master's degree in teaching English as a second language; and the 1975 agreement with Egypt, by which on a five-year contract the University of California at Los Angeles is providing staff in the faculty of education of 'Ain Shams University in order to improve the quality of English teaching in that country.

United States Information Agency. Within USIA operation, a minimal portion of the time and effort of the Voice of America is devoted to teaching English, but without the guidance of an English specialist. A recent event, following the beaming of lessons to mainland China, was the receipt of numerous requests from China for advanced textbooks in English.

But the strength of USIA's operation is in its English Teaching Division. This functions in part through USIS libraries but primarily through holding inservice and preservice seminars by its professional staff, through cooperating with binational centers in conducting English classes, through producing appropriate teaching materials, and through publishing a pedagogical journal, The English Teaching Forum, with a circulation of more than 70,000 through our posts abroad.

Oddly enough, the Smith-Mundt Act of 1948 prohibits the Agency from distributing the Forum, which was established in 1962, to residents of the United States, so that students and teachers planning to teach English abroad, part of the very group the journal is aimed at, cannot obtain it until they leave the country. But Congressman Donald Fraser expects to introduce an amendment to the next appropriations bill so as to remove this anomaly.

Some hint as to the effectiveness of teaching in the binational centers when native speakers are employed appears in my experience in a high school in Teheran four years ago. Only two students in a third-year English class could converse with me; they readily acknowledged that they obtained their skill through studying English at the Iran-American Society center.

Agency for International Development. AID, though without its
own English teaching specialists, has an imposing record of past
accomplishment through establishing language laboratories, offering
intensive English programs to middle management personnel in
various countries, helping to prepare textbooks and other materials,
and making a long-range plan for regional English Teacher Training
Centers throughout the world. In 1970, for example, AID provided
textbook paper, books, and manuals in Indonesia, sent 400,000 English language textbooks to Vietnam, offered in Kenya both preservice
and inservice training for elementary teachers and supervisors, gave
Nigeria books and grants to improve English teaching and set up a
language laboratory at Kano, continued some support for its first
regional training center in Beirut, and funded the final steps in the
building of the center in Singapore. This second teacher training
center is housed in its own 18-story building, dedicated in 1972. It
has a staff of 12 besides two language experts each from the
United States, Australia, and New Zealand. It has training and research facilities, a library, research and publications units, a 30-
post language laboratory, tutorial and class rooms, and self-supporting
office and hotel accommodations intended to finance the building operation without further funding. The center provides a one-year diploma
course, a four-month certificate course, and a three-month specialized advanced course, all of which have been taken in numbers by
teachers from the countries of Indonesia and Southeast Asia.

And the demands upon AID continued. In 1972 Afghanistan re-
quested a seven-month national survey of English-teaching needs and
resources, Senegal sought an English-teaching center, and Yemen
asked for English teaching through the new AID mission there.

Most recently, AID has given Georgetown University a five-year
contract to set up and staff in Damascus an intensive English teaching
center for a limited number of government officials and for graduate
students intended to study in the United States. The total obligation
will be about $1,000,000.

Health, Education, and Welfare. The Office of Education for many
years has directed the International Educational Development Program, which between 1960 and 1975 brought more than 2,000 teachers
and supervisors to the United States, most of them for six-month
orientation and training experiences but some for a semester's advanced work at some selected university. This continuing activity
has in considerable measure been given financial support by the
countries sponsoring the grantees.

Peace Corps. The Peace Corps was not created primarily as an
English teaching project, and its initial position, indeed, was that if

Peace Corps volunteers were to teach English they could take on the assignment quite adequately since they were native speakers of English. By 1964, however, repeated suggestions from NACTEFL led to at least some acceptance of the view that a certain measure of professionalism was required. Most of the Corps' 10,000 trainees that year participated in 35 training programs that had at least a minimal English as a foreign language component.

By 1970 the Peace Corps had five professional English language teaching specialists. By 1974 the number had grown to seven, and the eastern Africa programs had become largely concerned with English teaching, with 378 volunteers teaching in schools and preparing teachers in teacher-training colleges in 13 French-speaking countries. The Peace Corps then also taught English in six African countries that formerly were British colonies. In addition, there were 650 English-teaching volunteers in Afghanistan, Iran, Korea, Tunisia, Yemen, and elsewhere, and the Peace Corps conducted English workshops in Fiji, Thailand, and Malaysia. An oft-repeated suggestion from NACTEFL led to the creation of an English-teaching clearinghouse in Washington in 1975.

Department of Defense. Different from the other agencies is the Defense Language Institute of the Department of Defense, charged as it is with providing specifically targeted intensive English instruction for foreign military personnel. The numbers of participants are staggering in this largest single English-teaching operation in the world. In 1964, 100,000 military personnel studied English in this program either here or in their own countries. With the trend toward local country instruction, the number brought to the United States has diminished, but in 1976 more than 6,000 military personnel studied here, nearly all at Lackland Air Force Base in Texas. Some of these received further instruction intended to prepare them to serve as teachers of English in their own armed forces.

Not to be overlooked in this broad picture of our English teaching job abroad is the value of cooperation that has come from two kinds of sources. One is the British Council, which has accepted the uniqueness of the joint mission of the two countries. The Council and the United States Information Agency have held four conferences, two in England and two here, in addition to their mutual participation in the Tenth Anniversary Conference of the Center for Applied Linguistics in 1972. They have jointly produced a program on British and American English for the Voice of America and BBC. Beginning in 1974 and continuing for two additional years, they cooperated with the Ford Foundation in supporting and staffing a linguistic institute in Cairo. They have joined in support of a program at the University of Leeds to train African specialists in the teaching of English. Throughout the world they have consistently cooperated in about 15 percent of the short-term USIA training courses, especially in countries without institutionalized programs. They have cooperated in several respects in India, as in the regional center in Hyderabad, and likewise in undertaking the English teaching survey in Jordan in 1974.

The other cooperating resource has been the foundations, chiefly the Ford Foundation and the Rockefeller Foundation, but also the Asia Foundation with its support of grants for American linguists and specialists to conduct seminars and produce materials in Japan. The Ford Foundation has undertaken several major projects, notably a long-term teacher-training and materials-preparation program in Indonesia and that of the Cornell University Center in Rome. The Rockefeller Foundation was equally active with a somewhat similar program carried out in the Philippines by the University of California at Los Angeles. Rockefeller also joined the Department of State in enabling nine Egyptian college teachers of English to obtain doctorates in linguistics at three American universities, and 20 members of the English inspectorate in Egypt to obtain the M. A. degree in linguistics at Brown University.

Clearly, the demand for English on a worldwide level has steadily grown. Even in a huge area where we have no responsibility for it, the Soviet Union, the demand is tremendous. Last year 1, 100, 000 students in the USSR were learning English. Two weeks ago, at the State University of Samarkand in Uzbekistan, I found a 17-person English teaching staff that is preparing 200 English teachers and translators each year. It is particularly relevant that a current trend in English pedagogy is harmonious with this worldwide demand, the trend away from the sterile and boring drills of a quarter-century ago toward materials providing at least a minimum of immediate communicative competence. This recognizes the demand not primarily for the English of Shakespeare or Dickens but immediately for the English that enables people to read what is important for their jobs, to talk with others when their own languages are mutually unintelligible, to understand English radio and television broadcasts. Even in the eight African countries that once were French colonies, the demand is such that in 1975 ten American lecturers were sent to their universities.

All this sounds good. We seem to be meeting our responsibility. But this is the 'up' in the life of TEFL in the American role in global interdependence. Now let us look at the contrast between the bright picture of the past, on the one hand, and on the other, what is happening in the present and will continue in the future, unless a drastic reversal of policy occurs. This is, unhappily, the 'down'.

You will remember that in 1965 President Johnson accorded teaching English abroad high priority among the nation's international responsibilities. Since then, not one American president has made a similar commitment. In 1962 and 1963, two assistant secretaries of state with this area of concern pledged high priority in their statements at meetings of the National Advisory Council on Teaching English as a Foreign Language. Up to the most recent NACTEFL session in 1975, not one of their successors has followed that precedent.

It may be futile to dispute which comes first, the egg or the chicken, but it was the Congress following Johnson's administration which began the drop in appropriations leading to the present unhappy situation. And without a presidential directive for English-teaching priority and without a specific charge and appropriation by Congress, agency and department heads have themselves tended--for whatever reasons and under whatever pressures--to accord lower and lower priority to the teaching of English as being less visible than orchestras, ballet troupes, and theatrical casts. We are now shirking our global responsibility. If those are harsh words, let us do what politicians like to tell us to do: 'Let's look at the record'.

In 1966-67, the high point, the State Department was able to provide 199 grants to Americans going abroad and 124 to grantees coming here, a total of 323. The following year the total dropped to 224. Such a shift attracted the attention of the United States Advisory Commission on International Education and Cultural Affairs, which in its report to Congress in January, 1969, declared strongly: 'These fluctuations . . . show the lack of a firm belief in Government-sponsored international and cultural programs which is unbecoming a great nation.' But the decline in the support of English as a foreign language continued until, by 1975-76, only 103 Americans received grants to go abroad and only 36 grantees came from other countries; this total of 139 constituted a drop of 57 percent in ten years at a time when the demand for grants and grantees had grown past all expectations.

More critical is the situation in AID. True, a decline had occurred earlier because of the general decrease in all foreign assistance from 3 percent of the GNP under the Marshall Plan to only .25 percent today. But in 1973 and 1975, Congress redirected the assistance function of AID so as to benefit the poor in less developed countries and to provide bilingual education with the national language as the target for speakers of local tongues, such as Guarani in Paraguay. This allocation of funds, however, overlooked the fact that even in such programs, supervisors, foremen, and others above the manual labor level would profit from the ability to read English directions and instructions and to communicate with English-speaking consultants. The result is simply that with the present Congress AID projects for teaching English as a foreign language have quite disappeared, and will not reappear without a change in direction authorized and supported by Congress. We have seen the collapse of AID's magnificent and wholly practical dream of establishing six great teacher training centers around the world. Now only some deficit funding goes to Beirut and, in 1975-76, $70,000 to Singapore for scholarships.

I turn now to USIA. At the Washington joint conference with the British Council in 1959 George Allen, the then USIA director, said: 'If any members of Congress wanted to up our program by $50,000,000 during the next year, I would say: "Yes, I can use that. I could use it on English language teaching".'

But despite the importance Ambassador Allen perceived, the English Teaching Division has since then been seen not as central in the Agency but rather as having only a supporting role in USIA's concern with the arts, American culture, and 'the American message', whatever that may be. It is not unfair to suggest that its fortunes within the Agency have fluctuated not only in accord with legislative funding but also in accord with the personal enthusiasms of any given director. Thus a recent director thought so little of the division that by fiat he simply abolished the Agency's prestigious English Teaching Advisory Panel, in utter disregard of the invaluable professional counsel its members had regularly provided. And, although the Agency itself has suffered budget cuts in Congress, the English Teaching Division has suffered out of all proportion, since its share of the appropriation is allocated within the Agency, where it is now low man on the totem pole. That share has dropped steadily every biennium from a high of nearly $3,000,000 in FY1967 to only a half million in FY1975. Since these figures ignore inflation, the actual decrease in ten years was more than 60 percent, an even greater reduction than the State Department experienced. And because Washington headquarters staff could not easily be cut very much, the most stringent decrease was overseas, with a drop from $2,250,000 in FY1967 to only a little more than $800,000 in FY1976.

Inevitably, the USIA personnel situation overseas soon became tragic. In 1952 Bangkok's binational center had four Agency specialists for 800 students; today it has only one Agency-assigned specialist for 6,000 students. In Latin America the mid-50s number of more than 50 base-assigned English teaching specialists had already been sliced to 22 by 1961; in 1965 it was 12; in 1969 it was 4; today there are none! At present there are only 19 such specialists, six overseas as directors of courses (one in Bangkok, two in Teheran, one in Rabat, one in Kinshasa, one as the English teaching officer in Warsaw), and 13 in Washington. In a desperate attempt to retain some vestige of consulting momentum, five of these 13 are now assigned as traveling consultants; they spend nearly all their time going from post to post overseas, trying as best they can to help the non-Agency local staff, American and indigenous, to maintain teaching standards.

If the present director had the $50,000,000 which Ambassador Allen whimsically fantasized in 1959, it would not be hard to suggest how he might spend it. He could hire 35 English teaching specialists to fill what is well nigh a void. He could set up a network of cooperating centers providing service to homogeneous geographic areas, e.g. two in South America, two in Europe, one for the Maghreb and the Arab Middle East, and one in East Asia. He could hire auxiliary specialists for each center to work with local subcenters. He could hire a permanent specialist for each regional center, to be stationed in Washington as a resource person for that region. He could even hire an associate editor for the English Teaching Forum, now a harassed one-editor operation. But I, too, fantasize.

The foreign educational exchange program also has been hard hit. Last year's Office of Education report to NACTEFL revealed that the number of grants for study in the United States has dropped from the former 90 a year to 29 in 1972, 16 in 1973, ten in 1974, and only four this past academic year. For Americans going abroad the number of grants has dropped from 151 in FY1963 to only 20 this past year—and 19 of them were assigned to West Germany.

For me a climax to this sequence came a week ago today, when a telephone call from the Center for Applied Linguistics reported that, despite its having been created with primary concern for English teaching abroad, its financial situation and a shift in priorities no longer allow its funding the annual meeting of NACTEFL with government agency representatives.

Let us spare ourselves further grim details of this extraordinary holocaust, of this shameful failure to carry our share of the burden jointly assumed with Great Britain. USIA's six English teaching specialists contrast only too sharply with the British Council's 42. The British Council outspends USIA by a ratio of 4 to 1 in its support of English language teaching. But the competition is not with the British; they are our colleagues. Where we fail, and where private school operators and contractors (some good and some very bad) do not meet the need, other countries move in. France has greatly accelerated its French teaching abroad; Germany is likewise moving ahead; Russia is stressing the teaching of Russian as an international language.

Will Congress and agency administrations reverse this tragic trend? Will there be a desperately needed linguistics adviser to the President of the United States? Will NACTEFL gain support from government agencies so as to continue its professional service to them? I cannot predict, but we can be sure that unless this trend is reversed, unless we once more rise to assume our international responsibility, the effect will be to weaken the effectiveness of international communication for peaceful understanding and to militate against the establishment of world order.

COLLOQUIA

NEW DIRECTIONS IN
COLLEGE LANGUAGE PROGRAMS:
A FRAMEWORK FOR DISCUSSIONS

HOWARD B. ALTMAN
University of Louisville

'Every body continues in its state of rest, or of uniform motion in a right line, unless it is compelled to change that state by forces impressed upon it.' So reads Sir Isaac Newton's First Law of Motion, published in 1687 in his Philosophiae Naturalis Principia Mathematica. This law seems as valid in its application to the corporate body of a college or university foreign language department as in its application to the celestial bodies which occupied Newton's lifelong interest.

There have been many changes in college and university foreign language programs in the past decade. Some of these changes reflect new directions for foreign language departments and departmental curricula; some do not. Some changes are matters of form, a rearrangement in some way of the curricular and pedagogical elements; others are matters of emphasis, a stressing or restressing of one element over others; and still others are matters of content, a redefinition of the substance of foreign language teaching and learning.

Let us begin by exploring the bases for the development of the foreign language curriculum in American colleges and universities. We can identify at least five major approaches to curriculum.

(1) The 'Monkey See, Monkey Do' Approach. Since the Foreign Language Department at Upstart University is offering a course in Spanish Revolutionary Literature (SP 623), the faculty of the department at Prestige Valley State College feels it should offer a comparable course. In this way departments tend to pattern their curricula after those of other departments. The fact that Spanish Revolutionary Literature is offered at Upstart University provides

the course with a kind of academic face validity and assures imitation by other institutions.

(2) The 'Professorial Hegemony' Approach. Faculty members prefer to teach courses in their areas of specialization or of special interest. The addition of a new faculty member to the departmental roster almost guarantees that, within the next year or two, that professor will be arguing for the inclusion of his or her dissertation topic as a course in the curriculum, and preferably a required course.

(3) The 'Task Analysis' Approach. An increasing number of enlightened foreign language departments is developing courses and curricula to prepare students for what they are eventually going to be doing after graduation. Sometimes this entails surveying the 'user agencies' of our graduates, if I may be permitted a military term, in an effort to learn what courses students need to be adequately prepared for their future careers. The 'task analysis' approach is a more recent phenomenon and implies recognition of the multiple and varied goals of foreign language and literature study. This is a marked improvement, it seems to me, from the conception of yesteryear, when such a 'task analysis' would have been unthinkable. After all, the traditional goal of the undergraduate foreign language curriculum was unambiguous: to prepare the graduate to enter the graduate foreign language curriculum.

(4) The 'Performance Curriculum' Approach. This approach is related to the 'task analysis' approach and involves developing courses to meet specific performance objectives which themselves are extensions of the philosophic raison d'être of the foreign language department. Carried to extreme it results in a 'systems approach' to the foreign language curriculum, a phenomenon against which many humanists have railed in recent years. Though systems thinking is unpopular among foreign language experts in the United States, it is strongly endorsed by many European applied linguists and language teachers and is the basis for the new functional-notional syllabus design of the Council of Europe.

(5) The 'Consumer Interest' Approach. Numerous studies of motivation by Lambert and his associates have made us aware that students' interests in foreign language study are as diverse as their aptitudes. To attract and hold a clientele in the post-language requirement era, many foreign language departments have innovated. Courses and programs have been developed to meet the real interests of students. As Rivers has suggested, courses have been tailored to fit the person--not the image. [1] Though more conservative members of our profession have viewed these efforts as little short of prostitution, the trend toward student-centered foreign language programs is very much alive in college and university departments today.

Less than a decade ago, in 1968, in the first <u>ACTFL Review of Foreign Language Education,</u> Bela Banathy surveyed 'Current Trends in College [Foreign Language] Curriculum'. Banathy isolated three major trends in the college foreign language curriculum of the late 1960s, as reflected in the writings and speeches of members of our profession. 'To serve international understanding through the learning of foreign languages' was one main goal in this survey. A second goal was the recognition of 'the vital role of culture' in the foreign language program. And the third goal revealed in Banathy's survey was 'a reexamination of the audio-lingual goal'.[2] If the lion's share of the professional writings in Banathy's survey--some 108 books and articles in all--revolves about the main themes suggested here, it is interesting to note that, almost a decade later, college and university foreign language faculty are still talking and writing about the same themes. The themes of the late 1960s, however, though they still exist today, represent only part of the concerns of contemporary faculty in language departments, as we shall see shortly.

Curricular reform in foreign language departments, and in higher education in general, has been manifested in the following seven elements.

(1) Temporal rearrangements. This entails modification of the traditional academic calendar. In college and university foreign language departments such modifications have been labeled mini-courses, weekend language retreats, immersion courses, intensive courses, and the like. In each case the traditional temporal parameters of the curriculum have been altered; either the length of the course--i. e. the number of weeks--has been changed or the number of daily contact hours has been increased.

(2) Spatial rearrangements. Modifications of the spatial parameters of the foreign language curriculum have been reflected in directions such as study abroad programs, language camps, junior year abroad programs, utilizing community populations as the locus for foreign language learning, off-campus experiences of various kinds, and the like. In each case the curriculum is learned in a setting other than the traditional or traditionally furnished foreign language classroom.

(3) Modifications with groups of various sizes. Changes in the traditional whole-class concept of foreign language teaching have been reflected in directions such as individualized language programs, small-group conversation practice, multisection lectures coupled with individual or small-group tutorials and practice sessions, and the like. Groups may be formed on the basis of aptitude, of special interests, or of special needs (e. g. remedial work).

(4) Interdisciplinary study. In college and university foreign language programs, this has been manifested in modifications such as

the teaching of history or biology in a language other than English, business- or commerce-oriented language courses, seminars with titles such as 'The theme of war as viewed in art, music, and literature', ethnic studies and foreign language learning, and the like.

(5) Media-based curricula. Experimentation with curricular forms based on media abounds in college and university foreign language programs. Computer-based, computer-managed, and computer-assisted foreign language courses have been described in the literature for the last decade, and despite the prediction that the language laboratory has become our profession's Edsel, institutions of higher learning, including my own, continue to purchase equipment and install laboratory facilities.

(6) Modifications of sanctions. In foreign language departments, as elsewhere in academe, there have been changes in the systems of evaluating and grading student performance. Some institutions have done away with failing grades (and subsequently some have reinstated them); some faculty have switched to criterion-referenced testing and grading procedures. Variable credit systems have become a way of life in many individualized foreign language programs. Student contracts are used in some programs; these allow a student to contract in advance for a specified letter grade and an agreed upon amount of credit for performing specified tasks within a specified time limit.

(7) Flexibility of the curriculum. What these elements of curricular reform amount to is the flexing of the hitherto rather rigid definition and parameters of the college and university foreign language curriculum. The lock on the lockstep curriculum has weakened or given way in many programs; student-centered curricula, humanized instruction, personalized and individualized learning--these and other shibboleths of today have become realities in a growing number of language departments. The forms which new curricula have taken have developed to meet local needs and interests, and as these needs and interests change, the curriculum will likewise change.

If one can assume that the topics of articles in our journals reflect the concerns and policies of members of our profession--and, by extension, of foreign language departments in which they serve--it may prove useful to examine a list of these topics in an effort to determine what directions college and university foreign language departments have chosen to follow. For this purpose I have examined the 1975-77 issues of the ADFL Bulletin since this is, in my view, the major curriculum-oriented publication for contributions from college and university language faculty. Articles for the past several years have fallen into seven major categories: (1) innovations in teaching, (2) international education, (3) career-oriented education, (4) issues related to employment in our profession, (5) language teaching for special purposes, (6) new curricular forms, and (7) the defense and promotion of foreign language and literature study. Among these categories, several suggest specific new directions for foreign language departments. I will focus here on three: career-oriented language study, language teaching for special purposes, and new curricular forms. And by extension I wish to point to another major category not itemized here, but one which may be said to embrace the previous seven categories. I will label this superordinate category 'Concern for the improvement of teaching and learning foreign languages, literatures, and cultures'.

Although the infusion of the career concept into curricula, including foreign language curricula, has been practiced far more in elementary and secondary schools, our college and university foreign language departments have not been unaware of the implications of this activity for higher education. Reschke makes the case for career orientation in foreign language programs in the ADFL Bulletin and describes a pilot program in German for students of hotel management and business administration.[3] The American Council on the Teaching of Foreign Languages (ACTFL) has published materials and conducted workshops on aspects of career education in the foreign language curriculum with significant participation by college and university foreign language faculty. The career focus is not viewed as a replacement for more traditional literary and cultural pursuits; rather, it is an alternative, an option designed to attract those students to foreign language departments who might otherwise fail to appear, and an incentive to retain those students-- through the development of greater proficiency--who might otherwise abandon foreign language study after only minimal exposure. As such it is a significant new direction for college and university language departments, and the interest in career-related curricula seems to be growing daily.

Career-oriented language courses constitute one large area of what has come to be called 'language teaching for special purposes'. As Strevens has indicated in a recent survey of this phenomenon,

> Among current developments in the learning and teaching of
> languages, the change which appears to be moving at the
> fastest rate and which brings in its train the greatest conse-
> quences for learners and teachers alike, is the trend toward
> the learning of languages for specific purposes rather than
> for general purposes.[4]

Strevens cites various examples of special-purpose language study. TESOL Quarterly, ADFL Bulletin, Foreign Language Annals, The Modern Language Journal and other professional publications list many others. For example, Donahue's article in the ADFL Bulletin

entitled 'Applied Spanish for the Social Services' concludes with the
impressive claim that the course with this title now (1976) has seven
sections and 160 students.[5] Courses in scientific and technical English abound throughout the world, and our age-old equivalent in
foreign language departments in the United States, e. g. 'French for
reading knowledge', is nothing but a special-purpose language course.
Thus this 'new direction' is not really all that new, but its pervasive-
ness, its ability to retain learners by giving them what the learners
appear to want, and its focus in some cases on one or two of the 'four
skills' to the exclusion of the others, make this a center of attention
in many foreign language departments in higher education.

In any discussion of new curricular forms the phenomenon of
individualized foreign language programs looms large. Despite the
claim of some that individualization has proven to be a fad and is now
a dying fad, the facts support a different conclusion, especially in
college and university language departments. What has happened
over the past half-dozen years is that individualized programs have
taken on new dimensions, different manifestations from those found
in the literature of the late 1960s. Institutions continue to experiment
with flexibly paced instruction, with curricula catering to diverse
learning styles and sense modality preferences, and with conventions
such as variable credit, mastery learning, performance objectives,
and the like. The results in many programs have been quite grati-
fying; a majority of students has approved of the individualized program, on the one hand, and on the other hand there is growing data
to support real cognitive gain in these programs as compared with
so-called 'traditional' language programs.

Another new curricular form which has been popularized in recent
years is the mini-course. Mini-courses, as the name suggests, are
reductions in both content and length as compared with conventional
courses. They focus on a narrower theme, often one designed to
appeal to a specific clientele. At the University of Louisville, for
example, the Department of Modern Languages has offered mini-
courses at the third- and fourth-year levels for several years.
Each course meets for half a semester--i. e. seven weeks--and
provides half the normal semester credit. Topics may be conventional or unconventional, literary, cultural, even linguistic in nature.
In this era of demand for instant gratification from one's efforts,
mini-courses offer the learner a more concentrated and focused
opportunity and one which, should it prove to be not what the learner
had in mind, has the added benefit of ending after only seven weeks.
Mini-courses lend themselves to special-purpose language teaching.
Indiana University has offered a series of mini-courses to students
as part of its summer program for the past few years. These have
been extremely well received, for they allow summer school

participants to study a topic in depth and move on to another, perhaps totally different topic of their own choosing.

I stated earlier that the superordinate concern reflected in the professional literature today is a concern for the improvement of foreign language teaching and learning. In the forthcoming 'Report on Teaching' to be published by Change magazine, foreign language programs in American colleges and universities will be featured. The focus for the Change articles is improvement in undergraduate teaching. ADFL and ACTFL have worked together with the staff of Change to present a picture of representative outstanding programs in the United States. Among the directions featured in the programs to be highlighted by Change are culture-based exploratory programs, new methodologies, intensive language programs, career-oriented language study, individualized instruction, and mini-courses. The conclusion that a reader should come to after examining the Change report is that foreign language departments in American colleges and universities have taken some genuine steps to improve teaching and learning, and not without success.

In The Autocrat of the Breakfast Table, published in 1858, Oliver Wendell Holmes wrote: 'I find the great thing in this world is not so much where we stand, as in what direction we are moving. To reach the port of heaven, we must sail sometimes with the wind, and sometimes against it--but we must sail, and not drift, nor lie at anchor.' I think we may conclude that, in many college and university foreign language departments, our sails are unfurled and we are moving ahead in a variety of exciting directions.

NOTES

1. Cf. Wilga M. Rivers, Speaking in Many Tongues: Essays in Foreign-Language Teaching, expanded second edition (Rowley, Mass.: Newbury House, 1976).

2. Bela H. Banathy, 'Current Trends in College Curriculum', in Emma M. Birkmaier, ed., ACTFL Review of Foreign Language Education [Britannica Review of Foreign Language Education] Skokie, Ill.: National Textbook Co., 1968), 107.

3. Claus Reschke, 'Career Education at the College Level: A Modest Proposal'. ADFL Bulletin 9:1(1977).43-47.

4. Peter Strevens, 'Special-Purpose Language Learning: A Perspective'. Survey article in Language Teaching and Linguistics: Abstracts 10:3(1977).145.

5. Moraima de Semprun Donahue, 'Applied Spanish for the Social Services'. ADFL Bulletin 7:3(1976).29.

CAREERS AND THE
FOREIGN LANGUAGE CURRICULUM

WILLIAM E. DeLORENZO
University of Maryland

ROBERTO SEVERINO
Georgetown University

Introduction. The focus of this morning's meeting is on the
weaving of the career education concept into the foreign language
curriculum at the presecondary and secondary school instructional
levels. This presentation, which is directed toward classroom
teachers at those levels, teacher educators, and other interested
persons, deals specifically with the following topics: (1) a brief
discussion on the limitations and purpose of weaving the career education concept into the foreign language curriculum; (2) a response to
some misconceptions which foreign language teachers have concerning the weaving process; (3) some specific teacher and/or student
activities which promote career awareness in the presecondary and
secondary school foreign language curriculum.

Weaving the career education concept into the foreign language
curriculum

Limitations. The general career education concept as it relates
to all subject areas encompasses kindergarten through postsecondary.
During that time, the students are expected to progress through the
four stages of vocational maturation: (1) awareness, (2) exploration,
(3) occupational choice, and (4) implementation. [1] However, since
foreign language instruction traditionally begins at the secondary instructional level, there is little time to experience all four stages of
maturation. Therefore, current foreign language involvement in the
career education movement at the secondary level (junior and senior

high school) is concentrated at the awareness stage with occasional attempts to explore related opportunities in the world of work.

Additionally, time constraints in the secondary school curriculum, the fundamental spirit of the general career education movement, and the need of foreign language educators to focus on the awareness stage, direct our attention to foreign languages as an ancillary skill as well as a primary one. Surely all foreign language teachers must realize that language as a primary skill is limited to a select few: prospective language teachers, interpreters, and translators. This is not to suggest that these career opportunities be totally ignored, but rather that they be put in perspective in relation to the number of foreign language students who might pursue them. However, an ancillary focus on foreign language utilization permits our subject area to transcend all areas of study, both academic and vocational. The 'ancillary skill approach' permits us to serve more students who might be interested in careers in engineering, mechanics, medicine, law enforcement, business, industry, entertainment--in short, all of the 15 career clusters, as defined by the U.S. Office of Education and which are included in the Appendix. Indeed, an emphasis on foreign language as an auxiliary skill supports our profession's belife that foreign languages are a vital part of every student's education.

Purpose. Since the career movement was designed to permeate the total school curriculum, it is imperative that foreign language teachers do their part to adapt the concept to their subject area's goals so that: (1) students become more aware of the many career choices which are open to them and in which foreign languages are an added attraction; (2) students gain a more positive self-image by utilizing career-oriented activities to help them realize their capabilities, capitalize on their talents, and accept their parents' and others' contributions to society as vital and rewarding.

These goals of the general career education concept are humanistic in nature. Additionally, they afford the foreign language profession an opportune moment to demonstrate that the foreign language curriculum can indeed relate its goals to total institutional goals and priorities.

Responding to some misconceptions. After numerous workshops on career education and ensuing discussions with the participants, it can be concluded that the four most widely voiced misconceptions on the topic are: (1) that the fundamental skills would be neglected; (2) in addition to all of their other duties, classroom teachers must now act as career counselors; (3) career-oriented information can be presented in a 'one-shot' presentation; and (4) the career education concept is incompatible with the traditional foreign language course of study because of curricular time constraints. A brief response to each of these misconceptions follows.

Neglecting fundamental skills. This claim is erroneous. Indeed, the continued emphasis on the teaching of fundamental skills, culture, and literature is vital to the development of the utilitarian aspect of career education. If the purpose of this aspect is to prepare the student to utilize the language as an auxiliary or primary skill, then the teaching of fundamental skills and other content is vital to the course curriculum. Career awareness in any subject area is accomplished through the standard course content and activities. [2]

The classroom teacher as a career counselor. This task is not the job of the untrained classroom teacher. One major goal of career education is that it acquaint students with the world of work so that when they do make decisions, they are based on a background of enough experiences to make their decisions realistic. Again, this goal is accomplished through the regular courses in the curriculum. It is not expected, nor suggested, that classroom teachers conduct career counseling sessions with their students. This task is best left to trained personnel.

Career education as a 'one-shot' presentation. Career education is not accomplished in a singular presentation such as a mini-course, a learning activity packet, a 'rainy-day' lecture, or a Career Education Day. The concept should be an ongoing process which is incorporated throughout the teaching sequence. It is blended into the daily teaching process, i.e. dialogues, drills, displays, culture presentations, readings, field trips, etc.

Career education is incompatible with the traditional foreign language course of study. Secondary foreign language teachers often express the view that the career concept is incompatible with the traditional foreign language curriculum since students cannot be expected to achieve fluency in a two-, three-, or four-year study sequence. Such a view demonstrates teachers' lack of knowledge of a basic purpose of career education: to aid in the development of self-identity and self-worth as well as to enhance appreciation of the world of work.

The awareness, and even the implementation stages, do not require total fluency in a foreign language. Many jobs, as described in a relatively recent survey of Washington, D. C., metropolitan area industry and businesses, indicate that it is advantageous for employees to possess basic oral communication skills in addition to the major skill needed for a particular job. If further proficiency in any of the four skills is needed, postsecondary training, often supplied or facilitated by employers, is available.

Specific sources and techniques for combining the career concept and foreign language instruction. The following are selected suggestions for specific activities or sources which foster the weaving of the career education concept in the foreign language classroom.

(1) Prepare bulletin boards on careers. The displays should emphasize the place of foreign languages in each career which is represented. Bulletin boards may show a collage of magazine or commercial illustrations which depict specific careers; classified sections of a Sunday newspaper in which the teacher or student has underscored, circled, or boxed out those jobs which require, suggest, or infer the need for knowledge of a particular foreign language; an illustration of the career cluster wheel (see Appendix) which serves as a base for connecting specific careers with corresponding photos or magazine and commercial pictures, etc.

(2) Create learning stations where students, alone or in pairs, go to work with learning packets, games, readings or other career-oriented activities which are conducive to individual work.

(3) Utilize names and functions of various occupations in dialogues, drills, questioning, etc. One excellent source for adapting text material to incorporate the career education concept is the Prince Georges County, Maryland, Guidelines for Career Education and Foreign Languages, and Supplement 1. A complete reproduction of these materials may be found in the ERIC system under acquisition numbers ED100-158 and ED116-462, respectively.

(4) Have students role-play occupations and participate in simulated career-oriented experiences such as applying for a job, attending to an emergency room patient, handling a business call for an employer who has just discovered that the person on the other end of the line cannot speak English, etc.

(5) Have students comb the classified section of the newspaper for advertisements which require, recommend, or, by nature of the job description, imply the need for a foreign language as an auxiliary skill.

(6) Encourage students to conduct personal interviews with individuals in or around the community who utilize one or more foreign language skills in their employment. These interviews may be taped and played back in class.

(7) Invite guest speakers, possibly as an extension of the interviews.

(8) Utilize the target language to discuss family occupations.

(9) Develop career-oriented learning packets, e. g. gas station service, medical situations, metric system, etc.

(10) Encourage students to serve as language aides or interpreters to local visitors, businesses, public or social service groups,
etc.

Conclusion. The current interest of foreign language educators
appears to be focused on the utilitarian aspects of careers and foreign
languages, that is, the practical application of a specific language and
the use of one or more of the fundamental skills in an actual job
setting. However, the foreign language profession must not lose
sight of a second aspect of the career education movement--that of
promoting the development of an appreciation for work and its vital
role in the functioning of any society. Additionally, the movement
plays a vital role in the development of an individual's self-concept
as he/she discovers his/her interests and develops his/her potential
in the world of work. Given this second goal, foreign language
teachers as well as those in other subject areas must adapt and
utilize teaching materials and strategies which foster the development of positive attitudes toward the world of work and one's self
in addition to the development of marketable skills.

NOTES

1. Kenneth B. Hoyt et al., Career Education and the Elementary
School Teacher (Salt Lake City, Utah: Olympus Publishing Co., 1973),
p. 20.
2. Darryl Laramore, NASSP Bulletin, March, 1973, p. 94.

APPENDIX

Chart of the Division of Instruction
Maryland State Department of Education

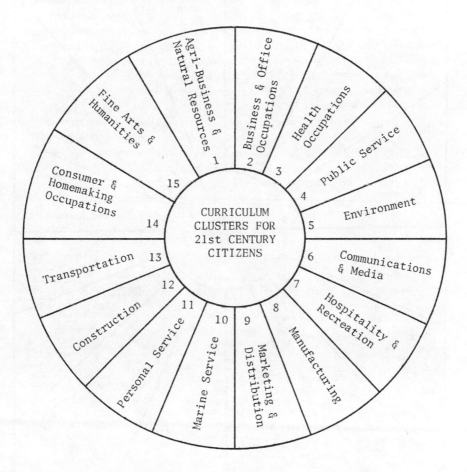

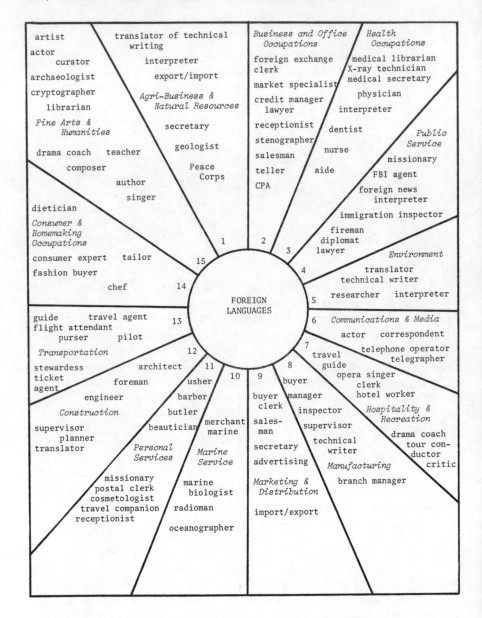

artist
actor
curator
archaeologist
cryptographer
librarian
Fine Arts & Humanities

drama coach   teacher
    composer
        author
        singer

dietician
Consumer & Homemaking Occupations

consumer expert   tailor
fashion buyer
        chef   14

translator of technical writing
    interpreter
    export/import

Agri-Business & Natural Resources

    secretary
    geologist
        Peace Corps

15

1

Business and Office Occupations
foreign exchange clerk
market specialist
credit manager
lawyer
receptionist
stenographer
salesman
teller
CPA

2

3

Health Occupations
medical librarian
X-ray technician
medical secretary
physician
interpreter
dentist
nurse
aide

Public Service
missionary
FBI agent
foreign news interpreter
immigration inspector
fireman
diplomat
lawyer

4

5

Environment
translator
technical writer
researcher   interpreter

FOREIGN
LANGUAGES

6

7

8

Communications & Media
actor   correspondent
telephone operator
telegrapher
travel
guide
opera singer
clerk
hotel worker

guide   travel agent   13
flight attendant
    purser   pilot
Transportation
stewardess   architect
ticket
agent   foreman
    engineer
Construction
supervisor
    planner
translator

12

11

10

9

usher
barber
butler
beautician   merchant marine

buyer
clerk
buyer
clerk
sales-man
secretary
advertising

Marketing & Distribution

import/export

manager
inspector
supervisor
technical writer

Manufacturing
branch manager

Hospitality & Recreation
drama coach
tour con-ductor
critic

missionary
postal clerk
cosmetologist
travel companion
receptionist

Personal Services

Marine Service
marine biologist
radioman
oceanographer

CAREERS AND THE
FOREIGN LANGUAGE CURRICULUM

ROBERTO SEVERINO
Georgetown University

WILLIAM DeLORENZO
University of Maryland

Under the co-leadership of Professors DeLorenzo and Severino, the workshop on 'Careers and the foreign language curriculum' met twice on Friday, October 7. Professor DeLorenzo's presentation at the morning session emphasized the importance of developing an early awareness of the unique relationship between knowledge of a foreign language and choice of a career, and dwelt upon the techniques currently employed at the high school level.

The afternoon session was held under the leadership of Professor Severino. The two main speakers were Dr. Mirta Vega, a bilingual specialist in charge of bilingual programs for Dade County, Florida; and Professor Alice Kent Taub, of the Modern Languages Department, St. Louis University. The other four panelists were the following: Dr. Jerry Ford, a specialist of English as a Foreign Language and author of articles dealing with languages and careers; Professor Guido Mazzeo, Chairman of the Modern Languages Department at George Washington University; Professor Franco Triolo, Professor of French and Italian, and Comparative Literature at the College of William and Mary; Mrs. Maria Wilmeth, a former professor of foreign languages at George Washington University, and, presently, Foreign Languages Curriculum Specialist with the Fairfax County School System.

Dr. Vega's presentation dealt with the languages problems of the Spanish-speaking community of Miami. She offered some solutions to the curricular aspect of the teaching of English, and presented a series of slides geared to help the Spanish-speaking individual learn the language of his adopted country.

Professor Alice Kent Kaub's topic was 'A foreign language: A key asset'. To use her words: 'there are many reasons why a foreign language enriches one's life: cultural, professional, personal, and aesthetic'. That day's presentation mainly explored 'the business and commercial advantages of knowing a foreign language'. For Professor Taub 'foreign languages are an added asset . . . frequently the key asset in a sharply competitive job market', and to better illustrate her position she presented a series of slides of classified ads taken for the most part from various editions of The New York Times. She firmly believes that knowledge of foreign languages will 'ensure a more versatile career and often, greater opportunities'. At the end of her conference, Professor Taub made available to the public a booklet which she had prepared in conjunction with Ms. Teresa H. Johnson, on this question.

After the main speakers' presentations, the other four panelists spoke briefly on various problems related to the teaching of foreign languages in this country, and their relationship to careers. Most of them emphasized the necessity of revising the foreign language curriculum, both in high school and college, to mould teaching of foreign languages more pertinently to the dynamic reality of foreign languages career related opportunities.

Professor Mazzeo thus summarized his ideas on the value of indepth exposure to foreign languages, whether they be directly related to a career or not:

In considering the reasons why foreign languages should be studied, educators should never lose sight of the humanistic values involved. Knowing the cultures and peoples the languages represent, with the resultant global or general views attained are of prime importance. The study of foreign languages helps us to achieve the ability to see the general, an essential part of the acquisition of a liberal education. Moreover, they help us know the world in which we live, and to realize the importance of communications among the parts of that whole. They help us bridge gaps between peoples and cultures, and to free us from what can be referred to as monolingual isolation or myopia. Language is the most used mechanism of the mind, and is basic to all thought processes. We should also bear in mind that most civilized countries stress the study of foreign languages far more than we do in our country. This is so in the number of languages studied, as well as in the number of years devoted to that study. The very fact that is so, makes it imperative that we make an equal commitment along those lines.

We do, however, have to face realities and consider the pragmatic reasons for the study of languages. We should furnish students with material giving information on job opportunities in business, government, and industry. One fact still remains, and that is that the person having a foreign language ability can achieve greater progress in whatever substantive field he may be engaged, and enjoys a far greater advantage over the monolingual employee. This is equally true in business, industry, or government service.

After Professor Mazzeo's peroration on the value of languages as an integral part of humanistic studies, whether or not such study leads to a lucrative profession, Dr. Ford said that invariably the mastery of one or more languages represents an enormous benefit on the job market because 'people who cite language training in their background are given preferential consideration in obtaining jobs'. Yet, Dr. Ford also stressed in his conclusion that career opportunities should not be the only driving force to lend value to language study. All things being equal--he added--'the candidate with a foreign language has an advantage over others. To employers, language training indicates a person with four desirable qualities: (a) higher intellectual training, (b) more cosmopolitan knowledge, (c) greater stamina for job obligations, and (d) more self-sufficiency for solving job-related problems'.

Excluding careers traditionally or directly related to languages, such as language teaching, interpretation, and translation, Dr. Ford cautioned that 'It is not only disadvantageous but sometimes unhealthy to present language skills as our number one asset. Employers are wont to ask "But can you type?" or "But do you also know how to . . . ?" There is a vast market for people with language skills, but most positions require a satisfactory working and applicable knowledge of another field as well. Consequently, we must conceive of language ability as a supplement, a secondary asset, rather than a prime asset in many instances.'

TRADITIONAL CAREERS
AND OTHER ALTERNATIVES:
EXPLORING THE WORLD OF WORK

ANN DAVIS-GERARDEN
JAMES I. BRIGGS
Georgetown University

This workshop began with an introduction to traditional career
patterns for language majors and a description of recent changes in
student expectations. Ms. Davis-Gerarden stated that teaching and
translation have long been considered the main areas offering career
opportunities for language specialists. However, both student
interest and job availability have changed in the past 15 years. As
different areas of the world become more aware of each other, many
new jobs have developed which require language skills. These include opportunities in the following fields: Marketing, advertising,
and management within business and industry; banking; radio and
television communications; publishing; tourism; social work; education; athletics; and all levels and branches of government.

As teachers and counselors of language students, we ask ourselves
how we can best prepare our students for rewarding and enriching
careers which involve the use of language skills. First, we must
instruct them in the development of superb linguistic skills so that
their level of proficiency will be sufficient to perform the tasks de-
manded of them in such jobs. Second, we must adopt a new approach,
changing our own attitudes so that we will encourage rather than dis-
courage students who are beginning the study of language. This
change in attitude is particularly necessary in light of the results of
a survey by the Modern Language Association which shows that 70
percent of the companies and organizations questioned currently do,
would like to, or expect to hire employees with demonstrated language proficiency. An even more interesting finding of this survey,

however, is that these employers indicated that 85 percent of the existing jobs within their organizations requiring language skills are not filled satisfactorily! We in the language profession have obviously failed to bring our students' attention to the availability of such positions and to attract the attention of the job market to our students.

Beyond academic preparation and positive reinforcement we must counsel our students to assess their own abilities and developed skills. They must also analyze the jobs which interest them to determine what skills are required for these jobs. Finally, they must match their own talents to those jobs which demand the abilities they possess. It is important for all students and counselors to remember that no job requires only one skill, be it language proficiency or any other. In addition, every language student possesses many skills beyond his language proficiency. These skills can and should be used to complement the language skills rather than to substitute for them as has often happened in the past.

The workshop continued from this introduction with a presentation on job search techniques applicable to language majors or, indeed, to any college graduate. Mr. Briggs affirmed Ms. Davis-Gerarden's earlier statement that attitudes must change. He asserted that the self-fulfilling prophecy is truer in job-hunting than in any other endeavor. Believing that the student will find a satisfying job practically assures that this will be the case. Beyond attitudes, however, there are several steps the student should take. The counselor can serve as a guide along this path.

First, the student should ask himself what kind of person he is and what kind of work he wants to do rather than what is currently available or 'What can I do with my languages?' Even the student who gets beyond this initial trap tends to go to traditional sources of employment information: classified advertising, employment agencies, and college placement services. Students who find jobs through these means are rare, however, so many students are discouraged and believe no job openings exist. Quite the contrary is true. Several studies have shown that 80 percent of all jobs paying over $7,500 per year never appear in these traditional places. The truth then is that jobs, many jobs, are open; but they are not widely publicized and are usually filled through private channels, generally by word-of-mouth. Once the student realizes this situation exists, he must prepare himself to enter what is called the 'hidden job market'. To do so, he must determine his career objective and concentrate his energy and enthusiasm on it.

In order to focus his attention on the appropriate jobs, the student should begin by considering the following questions. (1) What are my personal assets (skills, abilities, interests, values, education, etc.)? (2) What is my purpose or goal in life? (3) What kind of work environment would make me feel comfortable? (4) Do I have a geographical preference as to job location? (5) What are my financial needs and desires? (6) What lifestyle do I hope to develop?

Questions (1) and (2) are the most important, and they are also the most difficult to answer. To assist counselors and students in assessing skills, a skills/abilities inventory was distributed to workshop participants. Student volunteers were asked to check those skills they thought they possessed. After this task was completed, Mr. Briggs led a brainstorming session to determine what possible careers might be suggested by this information.

Once the student has defined his objectives, he should identify and research the organizations that meet his specifications. He should then try to identify the individuals in these organizations with direct responsibility for the work he thinks he would like to do. Following this research he should set up appointments with these individuals and interview them for additional information about his chosen field. This approach allows the student to develop important contacts within the field, as well as to learn more about it. It is his entrance into the hidden job market and will help him to focus his actual job-hunting efforts on the right kind of organizations. The person who conducts this type of job search stands a far better chance of finding not just a job, but the job he or she wants.

MOTIVATING STUDENTS IN
FOREIGN LANGUAGES

ANN A. BEUSCH
Maryland State Department of Education

GLADYS C. LIPTON
Anne Arundel County, Maryland, Public Schools

0. Introduction. What impels and sustains people to undertake
tasks which often appear difficult or almost impossible to others?
What makes them climb the Matterhorn; practice a Beethoven sonata
for three hours at a stretch; keep listings of baseball scores over a
period of ten years; study Russian, Japanese or Portuguese for
eight or ten hours a day? Motivation sustains and drives us all, yet
it is a complex and fascinating topic which even psychologists do not
understand completely![1] It involves a two-way interplay between
internal and external states which is difficult to analyze and which
may sometimes be in conflict. Internal motivation, or lack of it,
may arise from the need to belong or to be liked, the need to achieve
or to realize one's full potential, or an emotional need to avoid pain
or embarrassment. External motivation may arise from any number
of forces: the attitude of society and the family toward education, including the study of foreign languages, the climate and expectations
of the school administrators and teachers with regard to learning,
the attitudes of fellow students, perhaps the most important of all for
teenage students and their teachers.

1. Student opinion survey. Teachers who hope to continue to motivate their students in foreign languages need to know the students'
world. All too frequently, teachers do not wish to enter this world
themselves, because of their other interests and preferences. One of
the best ways, however, to become at least familiar with student

heroes and student activities is to administer a student opinion survey. It need not be elaborate. It does need to be searching enough to elicit specific names, titles, etc.

Following the student opinion survey, the teacher needs to revamp foreign language lessons around specific people, specific themes, specific ideas of student interest. If, for example, students have shown a preference for a particular television program, the teacher might announce one day that the day's work will focus on that program. Why not teach the future tense around future activities of 'Charlie's Angels'? Why not use as subjects of pattern drills the characters in Star Wars? Why not write fictional letters in the foreign language to 'Dear Abby' or 'Dear Ann'? Thus content can be covered in terms of student interests; applications can be developed more freely in the foreign language by the students; high interest content will surely help to motivate students!

The following questionnaire might serve as a guide.

(1) List your five favorite TV programs.
(2) List your three favorite singers and/or singing groups.
(3) List your three favorite songs.
(4) List your three favorite entertainers.
(5) List your five favorite parts of the newspaper.
(6) List the magazines you read.
(7) List the three movies you liked best during 1977.
(8) List the three most interesting activities you participate in at school.
(9) List your three favorite sports stars (and their teams, if any).
(10) List the five people in the world you would most like to meet.

2. Suggested activities for vitalizing foreign language classes. The Anne Arundel County (Maryland) public schools have issued a Handbook on the Teaching of Foreign Languages listing the following activities for vitalizing foreign language classes.

(1) Exhibit a current events bulletin board. Students search for articles and place articles on board themselves with a brief commentary.

(2) Provide a question of the day. Students are encouraged to find the answer to a question which will be found in one of the articles. Question is in English; their answers will be in English. If you wish, each student could draw a question as he/she enters the room and find the answer to his/her own question, or the entire class could be searching for the same answer.

(3) Plan for individualized projects relating to magazine/newspaper articles/TV reports. For instance, students who are interested in

the Quebec situation might research the origin of the situation, the problems encountered, the pros and cons of Quebec secession, etc. A scrapbook with magazine/newspaper articles might be kept. The student could present a brief summary to the class each time a new happening occurs. The scrapbook would be open to the entire class.

(4) Invite guests from many foreign countries where different languages are spoken. Guests may be invited to speak to the class on current trends, music, sports/games, political situations, etc. The class should decide what interests them most and prepare a number of questions before the visit. Follow-up activities should be planned after the visit.

(5) Display copies of current periodicals. Students looking through these periodicals will realize that language is actually used somewhere in the world.

(6) Publish a foreign language newspaper (very simple). It would most likely contain articles on school activities and illustrated comments and puzzles.

(7) Explore the number of different languages which exist in the world and where these are spoken. A class bulletin board showing the findings would be useful. It might also be interesting to see the number and names of countries where more than one language is the official language of the country.

(8) Teach folk dances of the world.

(9) Teach folk songs from several countries.

(10) Teach popular music and songs (e.g. some of the 'Singing Nun' songs are simple enough for the beginning students to learn a verse or two). Encourage students to bring in accompaniment instruments.

(11) Play music of foreign countries when students are entering and leaving the room. Also play it at quiet times, or when students are busy doing other things and can listen. Mix up the types of music played. If possible, include rock songs as well as classical music, music which is typical of the country as well as some that is a direct translation from English.

(12) Encourage tasting of foreign foods. Provide recipes and tasting sessions. Include bread, onion soup, crepes, petits fours, cheeses. Encourage students to try simpler recipes. Develop an international cookbook.

(13) Have an international table where students bring in an example of foreign foods.

(14) Teach food terminology which students are likely to hear or to see on a menu.

(15) Plan a field trip to a foreign restaurant.

(16) Plan time for crossword puzzles and word searches.

(17) Schedule games for teaching and reinforcing vocabulary (e.g. matching foods and meals).

(18) Display dolls from foreign countries. Students can research the costume (what is involved in the costume, the region it comes from, when it is worn, by whom, on what occasion, etc.).

(19) Develop a class bulletin board about holidays in a foreign country.

(20) Encourage students to dress their own dolls with authentic reproductions of costumes worn in different areas of France, Spain, Italy, etc.

(21) Try a 'Costume Day' where each student makes a costume of his/her favorite Frenchman, Spaniard, Italian, etc., and wears it to class. He/she might tell the class about the person and some of the interesting details about his/her life and times.

(22) Plan history/geography activities, such as 'Qui est-ce?' (Who is this?). The first day, only the picture of a person appears with the question 'Qui est-ce?' Students are encouraged to guess the identity. The second day a clue appears (in English); the clues appear each succeeding day until the fifth day, with each clue more obvious than the preceding one. At the end of the fifth day, all guesses are taken. On the sixth day the identity is revealed and the teacher/ class discuss the person and his/her importance. Vary the type of persons selected: politicians, scientists, writers, sports figures, actors, etc. Students may bring in their own 'Qui est-ce?' and write their own clues.

(23) Teach mini-units on places where the language being studied is spoken as a first, second, or third language. Try to identify those places in the world where there are language problems.

(24) Teach mini-units on famous Frenchmen, Spaniards, Germans, etc.

(25) Develop a mini-unit on the different types of maps.

(26) Plan a class-developed filmstrip/slide presentation.

(27) Plan a metric unit. Collect individual data (personalized, such as height, weight, size, etc.). Convert into metric units. Each student might have the metric labelling, which type of labelling is the most frequent (meters, grams, liters), and which products are the most likely to be metrically marked.

(28) Plan a mini-unit on foreign currency and compare the rates of exchange.

(29) Plan a mini-unit on postage stamps in foreign countries.

(30) Plan a unit on travel to foreign countries. Include time zones and travel times. Have students plan a trip, figuring out how far they will travel, how much it will cost them for gas, food, lodging, and meals.

(31) Plan units on European sizing (shirts, skirts, blouses, slacks, shoes, gloves).

(32) Schedule a unit on international road signs. Have students study international road signs and then make reproductions of them around the classroom and school. Make up class road signs and signs for public buildings.

(33) Develop a unit on shopping. Have students act out shopping adventures of buying, selling and bartering, using different money exchanges. Students will be able to practice shopping expressions in a foreign language.

(34) Plan a mini-unit on specialty shops along with different types of products found in each. (In a food unit, plan to have food samplings). Have students find products from foreign countries on supermarket shelves.

(35) Develop a ballet unit. Students will learn the French terms used. If possible, use student talent to demonstrate steps. Study ballets written by writers/composers from the countries being studied.

(36) Have a demonstration of a number of French, Spanish, German games (cards, sports, etc.). Example: piquet, boules, petanque. Invite a guest who can explain these to students.

(37) Teach students the names of the different fielders in baseball and famous players in other sports. (Use student experts.)

(38) Use a filmstrip/film which shows the various games/sports which are typical of the foreign country being studied.

(39) Teach the international sports signs for various sports used at the Olympic games. Examine the origin of Olympics. Work on a mini-unit on the Olympics.

(40) Have students find cities/towns in Maryland with foreign names (examples: Bel Air, Havre de Grace). Find origins of settlers in various parts of the state.

(41) Have students find out where their family originally came from. When did they arrive in the United States? Where did they arrive? What languages were spoken in the home? Does anyone still speak a language other than English? If someone does, he/she might be a guest speaker.

(42) Bring in ad/articles with foreign words underlined. Have a mini-unit on foreign words we use. Select topics and search for words 'borrowed' from other languages which are prevalent in specific topics (examples: the large number of French words in food, ballet; Latin words in law, etc.).

(43) Search for 'franglais'. Look through French magazines to see what words the French have borrowed from us. Franglais and words borrowed make good bulletin board material. This can be done with other languages too.

(44) Plan a bulletin board display of the families of languages.

(45) Plan pantomime activities, such as charades, nonverbal communication of feelings, and changing the tone of voice to change meaning of the same sentence.

(46) Have a fashion show with foreign language commentary.

(47) Plan how-to sessions in the foreign language; e.g. how to be polite in _____; how to scold somebody in _____; how to make a pinata; how to tell somebody's fortune in _____; how to answer a 'letter to the lovelorn' in _____.

(48) Construct a kiosk for school/class announcements.

(49) Have a flea market.

(50) Have an international postcard display.

(51) Have a puppet show in the foreign language.

(52) Have an international coin display.

(53) Have a sports activity, e.g. soccer.

(54) Develop a 'Let's travel to _____' slide/sound presentation.

(55) Develop a foreign language video-film cassette presentation of a familiar story or fable.

(56) Write letters in the foreign language, e.g. to a foreign student, to the foreign language teacher to explain an absence.

(57) Write a radio or television script in the foreign language and record/videotape.

(58) Write a travel pamphlet about a specific country in the foreign language.

(59) Write a narration in the foreign language for a famous poem, painting, or a piece of music.

(60) Develop a slide/sound presentation on sports in a foreign country.

(61) Design a book jacket for a foreign language book read.

(62) Make a map outlining train or automobile travel in a foreign country, with a tape commentary.

(63) Write words in a foreign language for a current popular song.

(64) Prepare a photograph tour of a foreign country.

(65) Select ads from magazines and newspapers to illustrate proverbs and sayings.

(66) Visit a foreign language school.

(67) Interview three people from foreign lands: (a) parents, (b) school friends, (c) local businessmen.

(68) Interview a friend returned from a trip.

(69) Interview an airplane pilot, a sailor, a traveling athlete.

(70) Interview a personnel manager of a corporation that deals abroad.

(71) Find three people who were helped by their knowledge of a foreign language in their professional career.

(72) Visit two neighborhoods; compare and contrast ethnic influences.

(73) Hold a debate on a United Nations' problem in the foreign language.

(74) Make a map of products from around the world.

(75) Find want-ads which require foreign languages.

(76) Develop a chain story in the foreign language.

(77) Have a role-playing of applying for jobs (in the foreign language) listed in classified advertisements.

(78) Write class logs and individual journals in the foreign language.

(79) Research the language resources of the country and of the school.

(80) Develop commercials and advertisements in the foreign language.

(81) Engage in volunteer community work which is language-related.

(82) Practice tongue twisters in the foreign language.

(83) Develop cartoons and comics in the foreign language.

(84) Have a 'brainstorming session' with groups of students (three or four in a group) to discuss (in the foreign language) things to do with, for example, half a cup of coffee in a plastic cup.

(85) Have students write a 'cinquain' (five-line poem) in a foreign language:

line 1 _____ (1 word (noun)
line 2 _____ _____ 2 words (adjective)
line 3 _____ _____ _____ 3 words (verbs)
line 4 _____ _____ _____ _____ 4 words (free choice of types of
words)
line 5 _____ 1 word (noun, synonym of line 1)

(86) Have the students go on an imaginary trip to Argentina, France, Canada, Germany, etc. for a month, keeping a daily log of imaginary adventures on the trip.

(87) Have students say (or write) in the foreign language: 'Happiness is . . .'

3. Working with the community. In a number of student surveys, it was found that the study of foreign languages was at the bottom of the student preference list. Many teachers have banded together to reach into the community in order to provide an extrinsic kind of motivation for language study. In order to provide a guide to teachers, one type of activity in one location is described so that teachers may note the procedures and apply them to their local situation.

In New York City, the Metropolitan Chapter of the American Association of Teachers of French developed a special committee to deal with motivation and recruitment of students. This Focus on French Committee developed plans to celebrate French Language

Week in New York City. Some of the activities planned were: a proclamation ceremony at City Hall; songs and skits in the schools; contests for students (posters, poetry, essays); exhibits of French artists in museums; distribution to the general public of a brochure entitled 'Say It in French'; buttons, bumper stickers, posters; a visit to New York City by the Mayor or Paris.

The text of the proclamation read as follows:

> New York City is a multilingual, multicultural city. As an international center for business and trade, it is the home of thousands of French-speaking persons and the center for hundreds of French cultural activities. New York City serves as host to world-renowned figures in the arts from many French-speaking countries. It provides a welcome for travelers from near and far, many of whom speak only French. The New York City Board of Education offers a large and diverse French program in elementary, junior high, and senior high schools, filling a genuine need for New Yorkers to communicate with speakers of the French language, to enjoy films, ballet, cuisine, and couture of France, Canada, and other francophone countries, and to follow the deliberations of the United Nations spoken in one of its official languages.
>
> Now, therefore, I, Abraham D. Beame, Mayor of the City of New York, do hereby proclaim the week of March 5-12, 1976, as French Language Week in New York City.

It is difficult to assess the direct results of such public relations campaigns to recruit new students. In many instances, though, such comments as these were heard in the schools: 'I never thought that French could be such fun!', 'I think I'll take French next year because I want to travel to Canada', 'Learning French might be useful in helping me get a job in an export firm', 'I never knew that French teenagers liked some of the same things that I did', 'I never knew that French is spoken in so many countries in the world'.

Some other kinds of community motivation are as follows:

(1) service in a foreign language bank--translation and interpretation service for the community;
(2) secondary school students apply their knowledge of a foreign language by teaching it in elementary schools;
(3) students work part-time (or volunteer), using their FL skills in hospitals, museums, libraries, etc.;
(4) students compile a listing of foreign language resources of the community;

(5) students interview foreign language speakers in the community;

(6) students develop multilingual first-aid guides for the community;

(7) students teach mini-lessons in the foreign language in libraries and other public places;

(8) students make posters for display in store windows, such as 'You need a foreign language', 'You don't know what you're missing if you don't study a foreign language', etc;

(9) teachers and students tour elementary schools showing skits, dances, songs, and other uses of the foreign language;

(10) students prepare greeting cards in the foreign language for hospitalized persons.

4. Are you motivating your FL students? Teachers may find the following self-rating scale useful.

(1) Do your students feel that they learn something every day?

(2) Do your students want to come back to the next class?

(3) Do your students feel that they can talk about themselves (e. g. their interests, ideas, opinions, and feelings) in the foreign language?

(4) Do your students feel involved in the learning process? (Do they contribute in various ways: listening, speaking, making materials, correcting boardwork, deciding when they need extra help, doing research, etc. ?)

(5) Is there provision for using the foreign language outside the classroom (e. g. calling other classmates on the telephone, preparing skits, etc.)?

(6) Do you keep up with the students' world of sports, rock music, TV, and growing-up problems? Can the students talk about these topics in the foreign language?

(7) Do you reach out to the community and try to get them involved in practical uses of the foreign language?

(8) Do you speak to administrators, counselors, and other teachers about the status (and success) of the foreign language program?

(9) Do you plan a surprise or something unexpected for the foreign language class? Do you plan unusual assignments?

(10) Are your foreign language lessons different in format, or are they always predictable?

(11) Do you use different materials, such as print, nonprint, audio, visual, audio-visual, etc. rather than just a textbook?

(12) Do you incorporate current happenings in the classroom?

(13) Does your classroom look inviting and interesting (decorations, desk arrangement, music, etc.)?

(14) Does instruction sometimes take place in another area of the school (e.g. teach imperatives in the gymnasium, media center, outside the building)?

(15) Do you involve parents and other interested people in international festivities? Do they share their experiences with the students?

(16) Do you encourage students to serve as FL volunteers in hospitals, preparing cookbooks, entertaining in nursing homes, etc.?

(17) Do you sometimes exchange classes with other teachers within the school or interschool, so that students hear the foreign language spoken by many people?

(18) Do you and your students become part of the school's important activities (e.g. FL cheers for a football game)?

(19) Do you 'recharge' your energies by traveling, or by traveling vicariously, or by using your knowledge of a FL in a community service, such as a FL bank of personnel?

(20) Do you enjoy your foreign language classes? Are you motivated?

Individual scoring is on the following scale: score 3, frequently; score 2, often; score 1, sometimes; score 0, never. Total the number of points and compare with the following:

54-60: Hurray! You're motivated and so are your students.

45-53: Pretty good. What are you going to do next?

38-44: Try harder! Maybe you ought to visit and observe a '54-60' teacher.

25-37: Do you hate to go to school in the morning? Now you know why.

Below 25: It's the pits. You need help!

NOTE

1. See 'Human Motivation' in Psychology Today: An Introduction. Del Mar, California: CRM Books, 1970, 147-160.

NEW DIRECTIONS IN HIGH SCHOOL LANGUAGE PROGRAMS

HELEN WARRINER
Virginia Department of Education

When I began collecting my thoughts for this conference, a first
decision was to alter the topic from 'New directions in high school
language programs' to 'New directions for high school language programs'. The change of a small preposition, I think, is significant.
Many conferences afford us the opportunity to examine the trends, to
learn the latest, and to become overwhelmed by gimmicks and gizmos
and all of the 'new' things that we ought to be doing. The professional
journals are filled with how-to or ought-to topics such as career education, communicative competence, and individualization. It seems
to me, however, that it is not the purpose of this one-time, special-
purpose conference just to provide information, just to give us new
techniques to put into operation on Monday morning. I believe that its
function as a singular conference is to provide those who have come
together on this occasion with an opportunity to examine where we
truly are and to refocus on our goals.

I could signal the direction for us according to my own orientation,
but I think that the process will be more interesting and the outcomes
more productive if we all have an opportunity to contribute. I shall
therefore start our discussion by identifying several issues which
seem to me to be worthy of our consideration, and then I shall open
the floor to a discussion of them. I shall also invite you to add to my
list.

1. In the early 1960s, the greatest revolution in language learning
ever to take place in this country began. Its complexities can be
summarized in a simple statement: the profession decided to teach
four skills instead of two and to give a new role to and interpretation

of culture in the classroom. Now, we all know that in education, revolutions tend to transform themselves into evolution; and progress is measured by degree rather than in absolutes. My question is, how much have we really accomplished in addressing ourselves to these comprehensive objectives, and what is left for us to do? More specifically: (a) Do all of us teach according to our beliefs? Do we really teach all four skills? (b) How successfully do textbooks reflect the changes and are they good tools to help us get the job done?

2. When I first assumed my present job in the early sixties, one of the most frequent requests to speakers and consultants was that they deal with 'articulation', the flow of students within the sequence. That has not changed a bit. It is still a popular request. The problem has not disappeared. A few years ago I thought it totally impractical to consider defining levels for the foreign language curriculum. Today, I am beginning to wonder if that possibility, that need, is not looming on the horizon, and I believe that I am beginning to hear some of us speak out for better curriculum definition.

3. Many so-called innovations, developments, trends, etc., are written about, workshopped about, and advocated in many ways today. Among them are individualized instruction, the need to humanize education, teaching the basics, career education, incorporating games into classroom activities, communicative competence, confluent education, the expanded role of culture, the popularity of fêtes, fairs, and festivals, and such singular topics as suggestology and the Silent Way. Can the teacher keep up? What does the teacher need to do to keep up? What attitude should the teacher take toward these developments? How can one prevent disorientation and avoid becoming overburdened in the midst of so many issues competing for the teacher's time and attention? Most important, what does a foreign language teacher do to be 'good'?

4. ACTFL's theme this year is 'The foreign language connection--from the classroom to the world?' Are we indeed connecting? How do students perceive foreign language study? If we are connecting with the world in terms of practical applications, why is it that college entrance is overwhelmingly the primary reason high school students offer for enrolling in foreign language classes? That is in spite of the recent erosion of that influence. Consider the fact that college entrance is an extrinsic rationale for studying anything.

5. In the 1960s we began to advocate the opening of our classroom doors to all students. How much progress have we made toward this

goal? We have a smaller percentage of students enrolled now than then.

6. I offer the last point which I want to suggest in the form of a statement rather than as a question. I think that teacher education is in shambles. Other than the fact that more young teachers have traveled and tend to know the language and culture better, I can see little progress in this area during the time that has passed since the early sixties. We have done almost nothing to improve their pedagogical competency. Anyone who has stayed in college for two years can get into the teacher preparation program. The education courses for the students, especially the methodology courses, are often taught by personnel who for many reasons are ill-prepared to do so; little selectivity is exercised in placing students with cooperating teachers; and they are graduated and certified on the basis of knowledge rather than ability. I have little hope for improvement as long as the education professors who wear the mantle of power are those who are the farthest from the reality of public education today and as long as there is as little concern as there is for teacher preparation. The same problem manifests itself in public schools and in local education agencies when instructional specialists and relevant inservice opportunities are the first items to be deleted when budgets are pared. Unfortunately, this concern for the quality of teachers may be more of a public lament than an issue on which we can have much influence for change, but it is a real issue, in my opinion. But I do ask, can the individual teacher have any influence on this problem? How?

There are many other topics that we might pursue in this session, but these are among the key ones which deserve our attention.

THE EFFECTS OF LANGUAGE STUDY ON READING AND LITERACY

GEORGE KENNEDY
University of North Carolina

RUDOLPH MASCIANTONIO
Philadelphia Public Schools

Dr. Kennedy opened the workshop with brief introductory remarks. At the afternoon session he expanded these somewhat because in the morning session it had developed that participants did not have a very clear understanding of the purpose of the workshop. Dr. Masciantonio and Dr. Kennedy understood that purpose to be the exploration of the contribution which the study of another language can make to verbal skills in English: reading, writing, speaking, and understanding.

The format of each workshop was for Dr. Masciantonio first to make a statement describing the program in Latin in Philadelphia offered to pupils in the fourth, fifth, and sixth grade schools of the inner city. Performance of Latin pupils on the Iowa Vocabulary Subtest was one full year higher than the performance of matched control pupils. He also reported on Latin programs in Indianapolis, Washington, Easthampton, Los Angeles, and elsewhere, and the positive research on the effectiveness of these programs in upgrading reading and vocabulary scores of pupils of all backgrounds and abilities. A version of Dr. Masciantonio's remarks appears in Foreign Language Annals, September 1977 ('The Tangible Benefits of the Study of Latin: A Review of Research').

Dr. Masciantonio's remarks were followed at both sessions by questions and discussion. Among issues raised were the differences between programs at the elementary and at the secondary level, and programs using Latin as the base language and those using some other foreign language. Dr. John Latimer drew attention to the fact that in the program in Washington, D. C., Latin had seemed to have a statistical advantage over other foreign languages in improving students' reading and spelling abilities. It was suggested that this resulted from the fact that Latin was taught with much more direct attention to its relationship to English than is the case in teaching modern languages. Other participants described difficulties in getting the cooperation of language arts teachers and the lack of recognition on the part of school administrators (to be noted also in Harold Cannon's talk in this afternoon's session) that languages are a part of basic skills. It was generally agreed among the participants after some discussion that language teachers should draw on public concern with basic skills and establish the relationship of language study to verbal development by encouraging research and experiment and by publishing the results--though all present agreed that contribution to basic skills was not the only benefit of language study.

Dr. Kennedy then read at both sessions a portion of the Report of the Advisory Panel on the Scholastic Aptitude Test Score Decline (On Further Examination, CEEB, New York, 1977, 27-28). The thrust of this is to deny a causal relationship between foreign language training and verbal ability. Participants in the workshop pointed to various objections to the statements in the report. The report denies that there has been a reduction in the amount of high school foreign language study in recent years, which is not borne out by some other published reports. The report admits that students who have studied foreign language attain higher SAT verbal scores (an average of 100 points higher after four years of language), but tries to belittle this achievement by noting that they also do better in the mathematical part of the test and that their average SAT scores have declined parallel with, but at a higher level than, the scores of nonlanguage students. It was pointed out that this latter statement did not seem to be true of students who took the College Entrance Examination Board Achievement Tests in foreign languages.

At each session Dr. Kennedy described the work of the Task Forces on Language Study established by the Modern Language Association and the American Council of Learned Societies with grants from the Rockefeller Foundation and the National Endowment for the Humanities. He invited suggestions for the work of those task forces.

ESL AND BILINGUAL EDUCATION

ROBERT LADO
Georgetown University

The program of the special interest group on English as a Second Language (ESL) and Bilingual Education (BE) consisted of presentations by the members of a panel, followed by questions and general discussion. The members of the panel were Dr. Rudolf Troike, Director of the Center for Applied Linguistics (CAL), Professors William E. Norris and Robert Lado of Georgetown University, and Dr. William L. Higgins of the National Institute of Education. Following are summaries of the presentations and questions and answers that followed.

(1) Dr. Troike

The issue of ESL and BE has been much discussed, especially since the Lau v. Nichols decision of the Supreme Court and its interpretation in the Office for Civil Rights Guidelines for school districts found not in compliance. The Guidelines indicated that offering ESL alone did not satisfy the requirements of the Decision. ESL would be a component of a BE program.

CAL worked with the San Francisco School District to meet the requirements of the Lau Decision, which was directed at San Francisco. The result was an ESL program for BE that was very different from what had been traditionally conceptualized as ESL. The traditional ESL program had been designed for adults and was transported to the elementary school by teachers who had never taught in elementary school. It was dissociated from the ongoing curriculum, and required that the pupils be pulled out of their regular activities for the special classes in ESL.

94

The ESL plan for BE did not call for special ESL teachers but required instead that all the teachers should be taught something about ESL so that they could integrate ESL into the curriculum through individualization, small groups, etc. Essentially, ESL in BE is to be taught by teachers in the curriculum areas. It followed that instead of State certification in ESL, the teachers should first receive elementary certification and then add ESL training.

Question: Should ESL training include more than a single methods course?

Dr. Troike: Three courses are needed: methods, language comparison, and cross-cultural comparison.

Question: Should the teacher know the native language of the students?

Dr. Troike: It is an extreme handicap when the teacher does not know the language of the students. Obviously, when there are multiple languages represented in the class, the teacher cannot be expected to learn 23 languages. You should then use supplementary materials and teacher auxiliaries that will provide multiple language help.

Question: Should certification include a foreign language?

Dr. Troike: Yes. It is very valuable. New York requires an intensive 120-hour course in Spanish for certification.

Question: What is the status of transitional programs?

Dr. Troike: As defined by the Office for Civil Rights Lau Guidelines, English and the native language are used until the student is able to be instructed in English. This, in practice, is a period of three years.

Professor Norris

My focus is on English as a Second Language in BE. There is a publication by that title published by TESOL (Teachers of English to Speakers of Other Languages), edited by James E. Alatis and Kristie Twaddell. Another pertinent publication is the Position Paper on the Role of EFL in Bilingual Education (1976), adopted by the Executive Council of TESOL and available free through that organization.

Originally, there was some distress at the Office for Civil Rights statement that ESL may not be appropriate for BE. The problem arose because ESL was used as a code word for one type of classroom procedure (mechanical mim-mem). Trained ESL teachers are not identified with a mechanical method. At the end of the Position Paper is a statement to the effect that the method should be adapted to BE, which is to be carried out in the dominant language.

A teacher of ESL needs more than a methods course to be qualified. TESL is a profession and as such requires training. To that effect TESOL held a conference on guidelines for TESL qualifications. They require, among other pertinent things: (1) knowledge of the structure of the student's language and experience in learning a second language, (2) a wide range of experience in teaching a foreign language and knowledge of the principles of second language teaching.

ESL belongs in BE; it is part of BE and requires high professional skills on the part of the teacher.

Question: In New York, there is the idea that an ESL teacher is a second class English teacher. Please comment.

Professor Norris: An ESL teacher is a special brand of language teacher, not a remedial teacher, and not a compensatory teacher.

Question: Should the ESL teacher be a native speaker of English?

Professor Norris: The ESL teacher must be a good model for the students to imitate, not necessarily a native speaker.

Professor Lado

English in the context of BE is different from EFL (English as a Foreign Language), ESL (English as a Second Language), ESD (English as a Second Dialect), ENL (English as a Native Language), and ESP (English for Special Purposes).

(1) BE includes culture. It is bicultural by definition, since the students participate in both cultures, usually that of the home and that of the school.

(2) BE includes learning content subjects through English as well as through the native language (NL).

(3) BE cannot ignore the NL in teaching, because the development of a bilingual/bicultural person is the goal and that means the ability to use both languages in their cultural contexts.

(4) Even young children use the NL to learn the second language. This is true whether or not the teacher accepts the NL of the student. Iqbal (1961) in 'A child learning a foreign language in England', reports that the child, for whom English was the third language, was lost in the total-immersion ENL curriculum until she began to ask in the NL at home, 'How do you say this? What does that mean?' in a bilingual strategy of her own. With that input she readily adjusted to her school environment.

In this connection, it is possible to misinterpret the otherwise valuable research on language acquisition that has been emphasizing the similarities in the order of acquisition of grammar rules by diverse children. It has prompted the idea that adults learn a second language the same way children acquire their NL. The misinterpretation is to conclude that bilingual children use the same strategies to learn their second language, ignoring the fact that they already use their NL to communicate and to learn.

(5) The fact that there may be multiple languages represented in the same classroom poses a problem for the ESL teacher in BE, but this does not justify turning necessity into virtue and ignoring the fact that each child's learning is influenced by his or her particular NL and culture. As pointed out by Dr. Troike, the teacher in such a situation should be given assistance in the form of supplementary bilingual materials and teacher aids or resource persons for those languages not within his or her competence.

(6) Early bilingual reading is a promising new approach to BE materials. Already two dissertations report successful biliteracy competence and bilingualism by first grade. One describes a case in English and Spanish by an English dominant child (Past 1976); the other an instance in English and Korean by a Korean dominant child (Lee 1976). Although Early Bilingual Reading is not exclusively a linguistic contribution, the linguistic component is a major one.

Comment: Two hundred parents in Arlington supported BE even when it meant learning a third language on the part of many of the children.

Comment: Bilingual education is not a one-way street. It also means that English-speaking children learn another language.

Dr. Higgins

Bibliographical resources in ERIC (Educational Resources Information Center). Each of 16 ERIC clearinghouses specializes in a particular subject area and is responsible for collecting relevant unpublished, noncopyrighted materials in that area. Of the 16, three are relevant to BE: The Clearinghouse on Languages and Linguistics, the Clearinghouse on Urban Education, and the Clearinghouse on Rural Schools. The ERIC Clearinghouse on Languages and Linguistics has materials on BE, bilingualism, bilingual problems. It is under the Center for Applied Linguistics in Arlington, Va. The Urban Education Clearinghouse conserves materials on Puerto Ricans. And the Clearinghouse on Rural Schools maintains the collections on Mexican Americans.

The 16 clearinghouses index 700 journals and publish the Current Index to Journals in Education and Resources in Education,

as well as 'fugitive' documents which are not readily accessible.
Five recent computer searches that have been and are available included all documents under BILINGU (to include bilingual and Spanish
'bilingue', English and 'Inglés', Spanish and 'Español'. Although not
complete--no bibliography can be considered complete--these biblio-
graphies include many items which the professional must screen and
evaluate for relevance to a particular problem.

A most recent addition to BE resources was the creation of a
National Bilingual Clearinghouse under the direction of Interamerica,
Inc., in Arlington, Va. At first it will service Title VII programs
only, but eventually it will broaden its sphere of service.

REFERENCES

Alatis, James E., and Kristie Twaddell, eds. 1976. English as a
    second language in bilingual education: Selected TESOL papers.
    Washington, D.C.: TESOL, Georgetown University.
Brown, James W., Maxine K. Sitts, and Judith Yarbrough. 1977.
    ERIC: What it can do for you/how to use it. Washington, D.C.:
    The National Institute of Education. September, 1975. Revised
    January, 1977.
Current Index to Journals in Education (CIJE). Indexes articles from
    more than 700 periodicals. Washington, D.C.: The National
    Institute of Education. Monthly.
Directory of ERIC microfiche collections (arranged by geographic
    location). 1977. Washington, D.C.: The National Institute of
    Education. January.
Directory of ERIC collections in the Washington, D.C. area: 1976.
    Washington, D.C.: The National Institute of Education. January.
Iqbal, Y. 1961. A child learning a foreign language in England.
    English Language Teaching 15.4.160-163.
Lado, Robert. 1957. Linguistics across cultures. Ann Arbor: The
    University of Michigan Press.
Lee, Ok Ro. 1977. Early bilingual reading as an aid to bilingual and
    bicultural adjustment for a second generation Korean child in the
    U.S. Unpublished doctoral dissertation. Georgetown University,
    Washington, D.C.
Lau v. Nichols. Supreme Court Decision. Syllabus. In: Alatis and
    Twaddell 1976:319-324.
Office for Civil Rights Guidelines. Task force findings specifying
    remedies available for eliminating past educational practices
    ruled unlawful under Lau v. Nichols. In: Alatis and Twaddell
    1976:325-332.

Past, Alvin W. 1976. Preschool reading in two languages as a factor in bilingualism. Unpublished doctoral dissertation. The University of Texas at Austin.

Past, Kay Ellen Cude. 1976. A case study of preschool reading and speaking acquisition in two languages. In: Georgetown University Papers on Languages and Linguistics, Number 13: Early reading. Edited by Robert Lado and Theodore Andersson. Washington, D. C.: Georgetown University Press.

Pugh, Elizabeth, John D. Embry, and Wesley T. Brandhorst. 1976. Survey of ERIC data base search services. Washington, D. C.: The National Institute of Education. June.

Position paper on the role of EFL in bilingual education. 1976. Adopted by the Executive Council of TESOL. Washington, D. C.: TESOL, Georgetown University.

Resources in Education (RIE). Abstracts and indexes recently completed (1966 to present) educational research or research-related reports. Washington, D. C.: The National Institute of Education. Monthly.

TESOL Guidelines for the certification and preparation of teachers of English to speakers of other languages in the United States. Washington, D. C.: TESOL, Georgetown University.

THIRD PLENARY SESSION
INTRODUCTION

ROBERT J. DI PIETRO
Georgetown University

The first of our three speakers is Mr. Harold Cannon, Director
of the Division of Research Grants of the National Endowment for the
Humanities. His career of government service includes the management of grants to humanists amounting to some $20,000,000
annually. He has also served on the National Council for Educational
Research of the NIE and has been the Endowment representative on
the Federal Interagency Committee on Education.
At present he is on the advisory board of Studia Humanitatis and is
a member of the American Philological Association.
Our second speaker is Congressman Paul Simon, of the 24th
District of Illinois. Congressman Simon has been in government for
two decades, beginning with his election to the Illinois House in 1954.
We in the language teaching profession have a very special friend
in Congressman Simon. Not only is he a scholar in his own right--
having written some six books--but he has been most influential in
getting established a Commission to Study Foreign Language Instruction in the United States. This commission will be charged with making recommendations to the President about what is needed if our
country is to adhere to the Helsinki Accords of 1975, signed by 35
nations, guaranteeing human rights and promoting international
scientific and cultural exchange.
Our third speaker is Dr. Richard Thompson, whose interest in
second language teaching dates from his undergraduate years at the
University of Pennsylvania, where he majored in oriental studies.
His specialty is Chinese. He is presently responsible for the administration of NDEA Title VI grants in language development and
for Fulbright-Hays awards.

101

LANGUAGE AND THE HUMANITIES

HAROLD CANNON
Division of Research Programs
National Endowment for the Humanities

On September 4, 1977, the Washington Post reported that the
foreign language program in Washington's elementary schools had
been severely reduced, when layoff notices were issued to 19 of
its 32 teachers. A deputy superintendent for instruction was
quoted to this effect: 'When it's absolutely necessary to pare
down you just can't carry on the payroll excess baggage . . . We can't
get burned if the kids don't draw well or can't appreciate sculpture
. . . We will get burned if the kids can't read or do math and science.
That's what really matters. These other things are nice little luxuries . . . Our students don't need complete fluency . . . Even if
you go abroad now, you don't need a language. The dollar speaks
louder than anything. '

Now, it would be wrong of me to blame any individual for these
commonly held sentiments; besides, I have a natural sympathy for a
bureaucratic colleague faced with a diminished budget. I cite the
article and the remarks ascribed to him only to illustrate what I believe to be a majority position.

The program in question has a 17-year history and was evalu-
ated in 1971; that evaluation report showed that sixth graders
who had foreign language instruction made greater gains in reading
English than those who did not. The Latin students, it said, did
better in this respect than those taking French and Spanish. I know
something about this, since the National Endowment for the Humanities invested public funds in the program to help demonstrate that
sixth-grade students who took foreign language courses would improve
their English skills; the project we funded was eminently successful,
but now the budgetary powers have spoken, and the program is a
shambles.

This sad little tale could be repeated across the nation, I am sure, with a thousand variations over the past decade. Indeed, William Riley Parker's homilies on the 'Language Curtain' still have a contemporary force. But this particular article in the local paper struck home to me since, on September 4th, I had just begun preparing my remarks for today; I had gone back to the talk I gave here in 1973 on virtually the same topic and asked myself, 'Has anything changed?' The temptation to respond to that question with a cynical negative is very strong, but I would like to resist it if I can, and mention just two things that have changed in our society in the past four years. First, the media have given great attention to the sliding test scores, and, as a result, the concern for literacy as a product of education-- the 'back to basics' movement--is extraordinarily widespread. And, secondly, the appropriations for the National Endowment for the Humanities have more than tripled, rising from $34,000,000 in 1973 to $111,000,000 in the fiscal year that has just begun.

In itself, neither of these events can solve all the problems of language learning in this country, but both afford opportunities that should not be ignored by those who care about the study of language.

The business of returning to basics is, for many, a media-created fad; but, whether it is reasonable, transitory, or supported by facts, it is very much with us in the minds of students and parents. At the very least, we should turn this popular interest to the advantage of language study. The newspaper report I cited a few minutes ago illustrates that the connection between language study and the 'basics' is not being made in the mind of at least one school administrator.

That the study of a foreign language strengthens understanding of the native language has been a cliché in the academy for centuries; now, in addition, we have studies measuring the compared skills of controlled groups to validate that cliché. But it has never been easy to persuade the monoglots of the truth of this without seeming to assure them that they are stupid and we are clever. When you add to this the tradition that language study is generally more prevalent in the schools where parents pay the bills than in those where taxpayers support the enterprise, you compound the difficulties of debate. Nevertheless, the ground for this discussion can be shifted to favor our side of the argument. Those hostile to language study rely on three principal arguments: (1) that such studies are peripheral rather than central to the educational enterprise ('frills', 'ornaments', 'luxuries'); (2) that the earning powers of graduates in later life will not demand application of skills learned in such classes; and (3) that their own monoglot training was good enough for them and therefore certainly good enough for others.

To counter these arguments effectively, we must first prepare our own. We must admit that the majority of our students will never find remuneration in the direct application of the skills learned in our classes; such jobs exist, of course, but they are relatively few and demand very high levels of competence. We must declare that education is much more than vocational preparation; being able to run a hundred yards in ten seconds may be a marketable skill for a professional athlete, but that is no reason for denying this attainment to healthy youngsters who will never earn a cent by it. Similarly, liberal arts education cannot be confined to the preparation of teachers. We must also announce our determination to make today's education better than anything enjoyed by previous generations of students--richer in opportunities and more demanding in content.

Much of this kind of thinking opposes current trends in education which may appear to be firmly entrenched; all the more reason, therefore, why we must 'go public' in the advocacy of our disciplines. The attitudes with which we contend in the classroom are shaped by society outside its walls. President Carter's endorsement of our position should strengthen our efforts and direct them into the public arena. We should all become vociferous critics of the media, active lobbyists with political leadership, prolific authors of articles for publication in the more popular journals. We should do this not to protect our own 'sacred turf', but to assure for our students enrichment of their lives and enhanced opportunities. Both by training and by professional experience we are admirably equipped with the tools of self-expression; but those tools never reveal their true sharpness while we use them exclusively on each other.

The public stance of the Endowment for the Humanities seems to me to support this cause, and the Endowment is always ready to apply its funds to such ends. Languages, literature, and linguistics are among the fields of study identified in the 1965 Act as humanities, and therefore as parts of the Endowment's concern. If money can help you in your professional purposes, we have it, and we have more of it now than at any time in the Endowment's twelve-year history. The Endowment considers unsolicited proposals in some 21 broadly defined funding categories; at present we are able to fund about 20 percent of the proposals received. It makes me very unhappy to have to repeat here a statement that I have been making with painful regularity for the past five years: we do not receive anything like a representative number of applications in your disciplines. Let me give you a current example. The general research program in my division receives some 170 applications every six months. In the current cycle of applications, there are exactly nine applications in the fields of languages, literature, and linguistics; that is not nine in each of those fields, but a total of nine for all three fields. I find it hard to believe that the research interests of the membership of the MLA are adequately represented by those nine applications, no matter what their individual merits may be. I note too that we have, in the same category, nine applications in painting and sculpture, and nine again in music and dance—this equivalence in spite of the fact that arts fields are restricted in our mandate to their theoretic and historical aspects! In the Division of Education programs there has been a lively interest in exploring this strange deficiency over the past few years; that division's current brochure includes particular reference to its interests in this area. Let me quote: 'The Endowment is particularly interested in receiving applications for . . . projects designed to improve the teaching of foreign languages and literatures . . .' (page 27, NEH Education Programs brochure, 1977/1978).

It should not be necessary to make such special pronouncements, but there seems to be some misunderstanding or reluctance in this constituency that requires explanation and encouragement. 'I knew you funded the Adams Chronicles on TV, but I didn't know that you could consider my research on the French medieval lyric.' 'But, I've never written a grant proposal before.' 'I thought you had to be at Harvard or Yale to stand a chance.' 'I'm not in the humanities; I'm in area studies.' These are some of the responses I have received when I posed my questions; they reveal a degree of ignorance, prejudice, and timidity I would not willingly ascribe to my colleagues, but they do help me to understand why I have nine proposals in this area rather than 99.

The Endowment is as interested in Homer as it is in Hemingway; other things being equal, we have no intellectual preference for the American over the French or Cuban revolutions. Our reviewers and panelists are as capable of impartial and objective judgment as you or I. Proposals are a kind of prose narrative no more difficult to master than the essay or short story, and very few of our applicants have any previous experience in this bureaucratic genre. Finally, if you spend any of your time reading, writing, and thinking, you are in the humanities, whether you know it or not.

I should mention two novelties at the Endowment, since one illustrates very well that the needs of a particular constituency of humanists are not necessarily revealed to us until we have a category of funding specially tailored to their purposes. In the spring of this year we solicited proposals for the production of annotated translations of significant humanistic works; all languages were eligible, but a particular preference for Middle Eastern and East Asian languages was noted in the guidelines. In April we received 241 applications requesting almost $10,000,000—virtually the whole budget for my division last fiscal year. We are funding 33 of these proposals at a cost of $1, 000, 000.

We expect many more proposals in this new category at the next deadline of December 1, 1977, and it seems likely that the 'one in eight' proportion of awards to applications will be maintained, if it does not become even more rigorous.

Several things have been learned from this experience: (1) that a great number of working translators are unaffiliated; (2) that many translation projects are underway, needing external funding merely to accelerate their completion; (3) that there are virtually no funds available for this kind of work apart from publishers' advances on commercially viable projects; and (4) that most completed manuscripts will require publication subvention if they are to be published in appropriate form and quantity.

The second novelty meets the latter need. Starting this summer, the Endowment began to consider proposals from presses and publishing houses to subvent publication costs of the products of Endowment-funded research. During the current fiscal year I expect we will be assisting in the publication of some 100 volumes in humanities scholarship--making life a little more endurable for scholarly presses, keeping the prices of these volumes at a reasonable level, bringing works to the reading public sooner than would otherwise have been possible, and, in some cases, ensuring publication that would not have been possible otherwise. Now my hope is that we will soon be able to expand the program so that scholarly works which have not previously enjoyed Endowment support will be eligible for consideration too.

The combination of these innovations is timely and by no means accidental. Whether you are in the translation business or not, these changes will have some effect on all of you. Many of you, I know, teach courses-in-translation and comparative literature (whether willingly or under duress), and you will find your materials enriched by this development. It is always possible too that a few of these 'English only' readers will be drawn into the study of languages. Meanwhile, translation of a certain kind and quality is being recognized by the Endowment as productive scholarship, and this should begin to make some difference in the ways in which the profession sees itself and in the priorities assigned to servicing the needs and ignorance of the nonlanguage student or of the general public beyond the classroom.

Our present difficulties are summarized in that concern: can we encourage and stimulate the study of language in all its variety while continuing to harness that study to the purposes of an essentially monoglot education? The needs of the greatest number must be attended, or those of the dedicated few will never be met. A generation ago, a bachelor of arts degree without some acquaintance with two or three foreign languages was unthinkable; now it has become the norm. Only drastic action will prevent the eventual disappearance of foreign language instruction from the secondary and undergraduate levels. Argument within the academy has been more than vociferous; it must now be directed at the tuition- and tax-paying public if any reversal of this sinister trend is to be evident in our lifetimes.

LANGUAGE AND NATIONAL POLICY

CONGRESSMAN PAUL SIMON
24th District, Illinois

I appreciate the generous introduction because I have learned in
public life you are never quite sure what kind of an introduction you
are going to receive. I recall some years ago speaking in Southern
Illinois to a convention about one of the books I had written, and the
President of the group, in introducing me, became unintentionally
accurate (something you should never do in introducing a speaker).
In describing my book he said, 'It's the kind of a book once you put
it down, you can't pick it up. '

It was a particular pleasure to arrive and find here someone from
Southern Illinois University--which is in my District, I hasten to add.
And, while I have great respect for all the other members of the
audience, obviously the most intelligent, quick-witted, and possessor
of other virtues is the gentleman from Carbondale, Illinois, who is
in the front row.

All of us remember when Nikita Khrushchev addressed the peoples
of the world, so to speak, and said to those of us in the United States,
'We will bury you'. The only trouble with that memory and that report is that he never said that. What he said was, 'We will survive
you', and because we did not happen to have the right language skills
at the time, we received a message that was not a pleasant message.
The original was not intended to be a pleasant message, but we received a message with greater overtones of hostility, in fact, than
the original. It is but one illustration of why we have reason as a
nation to develop greater language skills.

I hesitate talking to this group on the statistical evidence of the
need, because that is like carrying coals to Newcastle, but let me
cite a few things very briefly. They suggest not only language deficiencies but cultural deficiencies as far as looking beyond the borders

of this nation. The Educational Testing Service, a national service, recently found that fewer than half the high school students in the United States, when given these four nations--Egypt, India, Israel, and Mexico--were able to identify which one of the four is an Arab nation. When asked whether Golda Meir or Anwar Sadat was the President of Egypt, more than half picked Golda Meir.

Between 1968 and 1974, we had a drop of 15 percent in high school language studies. In 1976 only 4 percent of the graduating students had two years of a foreign language. And here we are talking merely about quantity; we are not even mentioning quality. I fear--and I mean no disrespect to this group, because I assume that this represents the quality of your profession--that if we started talking about quality, we would start narrowing those figures appreciably more. Ninety percent of the colleges today have no foreign language requirement. Between 1968 and 1974 the drop among college students taking foreign languages paralleled and slightly exceeded the drop among high school students. Today only one in 20 undergraduate college students participates in any course which involves teaching of either foreign language or foreign culture. Five percent of those who are now in teacher education, or are taking teacher education, study foreign languages.

Frequently we are in conferences with foreign nations where they understand us and we do not understand them, and obviously we are at a substantial disadvantage in any such bargaining arrangement. A good example of this was given to me just the other day in a case which I am unfortunately not at liberty to discuss in detail. The Foreign Service today amazingly no longer has a foreign language entrance requirement. I do not fault the Foreign Service so much on that because it is simply reflecting the reality of the culture of our day. If the Foreign Service wants qualified people, they have apparently made a determination that a foreign language can no longer be required.

Or, take an example from the Vietnam War. We did not have in the United States Government a single American-born specialist on Vietnam, Cambodia, or Laos, prior to our involvement in that area. We relied completely, or virtually so, on the French for our information.

With regard to the United States economy, one of every five manufacturing jobs is dependent on exports, one out of every three farm acres goes for exports. Top management jobs for U.S. overseas operations generally go to people from other nations simply because we do not have the language skills to fill those spots.

We have the International Education Act, which is a great piece of paper, but which has never been funded. The Fulbright-Hays Program--a great program in terms of 'real' dollars when inflation is considered--has dropped 30 percent in the last ten years. That, by way of general background, suggests that we are not moving in the direction in which we ought to be moving.

We have a commission in Congress made up of six senators, six House members, and three appointees of the President, called the Commission on Security and Cooperation in Europe. Basically, it monitors the Helsinki Agreement. Part of the Helsinki Agreement, signed by the United States and 34 other nations, states that the signatory powers will encourage the study of foreign languages and civilizations as an important means of expanding communication among peoples. As our Helsinki Commission met, it occurred to me that this might very well be a tool for moving in the right direction. And so I suggested to our commission that we request the President to appoint a commission of six months' duration, so that we do not end up with another commission that goes on ad infinitum, but that would meet and make recommendations to the President and to Congress about what should be done in this area of foreign languages. I received strong support on the commission from Senator Pell of Rhode Island, from Representative Fascell of Florida, and Representative Fenwick of New Jersey. The commission adopted my proposal and sent it to the President.

I met with the President. I met first with Stu Eizenstadt, the President's Policy Advisor, who was very receptive; then I met with the President. And the President indicated his offhand reaction was very favorable. He talked about his own language studies, and his wife's studies in Spanish. He mentioned that he had recommended to the Southern Baptists some time ago that they set up a somewhat similar commission to take a look at foreign languages, and he specifically mentioned the good work that the Latter Day Saints have been doing at Brigham Young University. I do not know if anyone is here from Brigham Young University, but the President of the United States is aware of what you are doing in the field of foreign languages. Maybe your trustees are not out at Brigham Young, but the President is.

About two weeks after that meeting with the President, the commission received a letter from the President saying that he would go ahead with the idea and that he was asking the Commissioner of Education, Ernie Boyer, to put the pieces of the puzzle together and make recommendations to him.

I have met on two occasions with Commissioner Boyer. We have gone over both the function of the commission and possible membership, and we have been in frequent contact, through his staff and Dave Solomon of my staff; we have also been in touch with others, some of whom are here in the audience right now.

A tentative list has either gone to the White House or will go to the White House within the next couple of days and I anticipate that within a few weeks there will be an announcement from the White House about the membership of the commission.

I am speaking now just as one member of Congress, because the commission membership has not been designated and the direction they will take will obviously be determined by the commission.

My hope is that the commission will take a look at the following problems, among others.

First, both the quantity and quality of foreign language education should be considered--and not just foreign language education, but the whole cultural field. I look back at my very meagre foreign language training in college; we learned how to conjugate verbs, but how those verbs fit into the life of another country was not even suggested in that classroom. Obviously, we have to do more than simply memorize words and pick up a language in a limited way.

Second, the commission must relate the foreign language problem to the economic and security needs of this nation.

Third, I hope we will face the very tough question of how to find jobs for people who have foreign language skills. If there are no jobs available for people who develop such skills, we are obviously not going to be encouraging people to move into foreign language studies. As a result of what has already happened, we have been getting some mail indicating an interest in this question, and it is not uncommon for someone to write and say, 'I majored in Russian and got a Master's degree, and I am now working as a secretary for a law firm because there is nothing I can do with my Russian language studies'. How do we effectively use the people who have developed skills?

Fourth, how do we encourage--and it is obvious that all of these things are interrelated--how do we encourage in practical ways those who have language skills and the development of those skills? For example, one of the many ideas under consideration is this: should we give an extra two points on Federal Civil Service tests for someone who has an ability to read and write or speak a foreign language? It is somehow ironic that most of the Immigration Service personnel patrolling the Mexico-Texas border cannot speak Spanish. Is this a rational way to run that kind of operation? This is the kind of thing that we want to examine.

How do we encourage the development of lesser known languages, not only Spanish, French, German, and the major, more studied languages? For example, there are 300,000,000 people in the world who speak Hindi and at present we have fewer than 300 students of Hindi in the United States.

How do we mesh what is a national need (or at least what I perceive to be a national need) with the reality of our present situation?

These are some of the questions that I hope the commission will tackle. I believe that the commission is going to have some very concrete proposals to make to the President and to Congress. And my hope is that at that point you and your colleagues around the country will become political activists. I am not suggesting that you start carrying placards or that sort of thing. But I hope you will do the drudgery that is not exciting, but that changes national policy: writing letters to members of Congress, to the senators, and getting your friends to do so; digging in and finding out what the proposed legislation is all about; and letting those who represent you and represent the national interest, know what you believe is the national interest. Let them know that you are not only articulate in a foreign language but that you are also politically articulate. I regret to say that the two qualities are not necessarily always combined in one person.

We need that involvement, if the commission is not to be merely another fine proposal that gathers dust. I really believe that we have the opportunity, or will have the opportunity, to move forward in a major way, to make a major contribution to this nation--and indeed to the stability of all nations--because of the U.S. position of leadership.

I was here on the Georgetown campus just two nights ago, debating whether or not we should approve the Panama Canal Treaties with one of my more conservative colleagues who does not think we should do so. As I listened to the questions from the audience (and I do not mean this disrespectfully to the Georgetown students because it could be Southern Illinois University or it could be anywhere), I was struck by how insensitive so many students were to the needs, hopes, and desires of those in other cultures. And if you think that provincialism is only a campus phenomenon, start talking to the Rotary Clubs and other groups and you may get even more discouraging responses. If we are to move ahead as a nation, if we are to do the responsible thing, somehow we must sensitize ourselves to the needs of others a little more than we have, and that means moving away from the 'they ought to speak English' syndrome. It means that you are going to have to help move us in the right direction.

As I hear and learn more about you, you are the leadership people who can help do that, and I think we are going to need you.

LONG-RANGE PLANNING AND THE FUTURE OF LANGUAGE STUDY IN THE UNITED STATES

RICHARD T. THOMPSON
U. S. Office of Education

Two Washington, D. C. newspapers, the Post and the Star, like many newspapers in this country and around the world, carried front-page stories recently reminding us that two decades ago the Soviet Union launched Sputnik. Even as that Russian satellite 'streaked around the shrunken nuclear-nervous globe at 18, 000 miles an hour', its impact was being assessed and, in plain language, the Russian scientists had beaten American scientists. [1]

What was implicit was all too soon made explicit--American education had failed, and the proposed remedy, the National Defense Education Act (NDEA), was on the books just one year later. U. S. Commissioner of Education Dr. Ernest L. Boyer, in remembering the period, stated: 'I don't recall a period when we focused so single-mindedly on education, and, when the schools were so linked to a national purpose. There was an almost electrifying awareness of the importance of education nationally.' [2]

The general provisions of the Act established that the security of the nation required the fullest development of the mental resources of the country and set forth to correct as rapidly as possible the existing imbalances in educational programs that had led an insufficient proportion of the nation's population into the study of science, mathematics, and modern foreign languages.

Title VI of NDEA (Language Development) provided funds for the establishment of modern foreign language and area studies centers; for incentive fellowships to encourage students to enroll in foreign language programs; and to help develop the needed curricular materials and foreign language textbooks, such as the early A-LM series.

NDEA institutes trained teachers in languages, in area studies, and in new methods of teaching. Language labs were set up throughout the country, and the students flocked in. This was the biggest thing to hit the foreign language profession since the Tower of Babel. Well, that was 20 years ago and how has the world changed, and where are we going now, and what about foreign language education?

We hear a lot about global interdependence these days. What possible relevance could this new concept have for foreign language education? In his recent monograph National Needs for International Education, Robert Ward, Director of the Center for Research in International Studies at Stanford University and member of the Research Council of the Georgetown Center for Strategic and International Studies, sets some of the stage.[3]

Try for a moment to think about our times in the historical mode. What impresses you most? What seems most seminal in terms of the probable contribution to a future that we can still perceive only in outline? Is it not some such combination of factors as the following?

Ours has been an age of new states. At the turn of the century some 50-odd such entities were generally recognized. Today there are about 150. Collectively these new states represent locales, races, and cultures that we somewhat ethnocentrically identify as 'non-Western'. Their needs, demands, and problems have come to occupy an ever-larger and more insistent portion on our agenda of international concerns and activities--and promise to do so for a long time to come.

Underlying these political developments is a literal explosion of scientific discoveries and technological innovations that sometimes leads us to speak of the advent of 'an age of planned invention'. As a result of the enhanced capacities and needs that ensue, the normal geographical ambit of our individual and collective activities has been expanding on a scale and with a rapidity that mankind is as yet ill-prepared to cope with. We are in the process of outgrowing yet one more boundary--the national frontier--long accepted as the natural limit of most, though not all, of our more absorbing and normal concerns and activities. One of the most salient characteristics of this process is the gradual blurring of the formerly more clear-cut distinctions between domestic and foreign affairs and the consequent popularization or domestication of the once-remote and professionalized process of making and administering something called 'foreign'--as opposed to 'domestic'--policy. Both government and peoples

are in the process of learning, and accommodating to, the
extent to which conditions and decisions 'abroad' are capable
of continuously and vitally affecting their lives, fortunes,
and well-being at home.

Was not even NDEA a reaction to conditions and decisions abroad--
the launching of Sputnik? And what about the negative impact of
World Wars I and II on the study of German, and the role of World
War II as a positive impact on foreign language education and area
studies? How many of the current foreign language specialists for
Chinese, Korean, and Vietnamese, for example, were trained by the
military language schools in response to the Korean and Vietnamese
episodes?

In her presentation Language and Politics in the United States at
Georgetown University's Round Table on Languages and Linguistics
1977, Shirley Brice Heath reminded us of the views of John Adams,
who, as a diplomat abroad immediately following the Continental
Congress' struggles to draft the Articles of Confederation, became
firmly convinced that 'the power of a nation's language correlated
positively with its political prowess'.[4] Adams was certain that Hol-
land had not achieved prominence because of a failure to promote the
Dutch language to other nations. Adams therefore concluded that it
was necessary to promote American English abroad and suggested
the establishment of an American academy of language.[5]

The notion that English is the international language of politics,
as well as of business and trade, is unfortunately still very much
with us today. In a happier footnote to this situation, the World Bank
is increasingly discovering that to carry out its business, it must deal
with the nations of the world on their terms and in their languages.

In a recent report of overseas activities by the Ford Foundation,
Mel Fox notes that language work overseas has shifted from a single-
minded interest in teaching English to a realization that multilingual
societies have acute language problems which are at the root of their
cultural continuity and their political, social, and educational development.[6]

Ward further notes that

...within the past four years it should have been conclusively
demonstrated to both the government and the American people
that this is not 'the American Century', that our capacity to
determine international outcomes has greatly diminished since
the early postwar years, and that, for better or for worse, we
will in the future be more dependent upon and more affected by
the policies and activities of other states than has ever before
been the case in our post-revolutionary history.[7]

In Education for Global Interdependence, a recent report of the American Council on Education, Stephen K. Bailey insists that

> ...what we do not know can harm us. Unless something is done to compensate for its educational anachronisms, the United States may well lack the expert human resources needed to steer American public and private enterprises through the dangerous and uncharted international waters that lie ahead. Equally serious, this nation may fail to develop the widespread popular understanding needed for the political acceptance of the difficult trade-offs which are emerging as the necessary logic of our living in a perpetual state of global interdependence. [8]

Sputnik, 20 years later, provides us with a truly 'global' reminder of our dependence on external events to serve as catalysts for needed educational planning and policy development.

It simultaneously forces a reflection on the nature of the interactive process of planning language needs and policy development and implementation. It will be the purpose of this paper: (1) to suggest a different kind of typology for language planning--one which is more oriented toward the development of human resources; (2) to provide a brief historical sketch of some of the major national language planning efforts in the United States; and (3) to attempt to forecast some of the implications of language planning for the future of foreign language study in the United States.

1. A human resources-oriented typology. In a recent reference guide for students of language planning, Joan Rubin and Björn Jernudd provide us with a convenient summary of some 30 views of the theory of language planning as currently practiced by the language planning research community. [9] Language planning (or language engineering) as a separate field of enquiry has newly emerged within the last decade and is in search of a conceptualization. Recent applications of language planning have focused largely, though not exclusively, on the developing countries. An underlying theme of 'planned language change' is common and includes, for example, such questions as the selection or modification of a national language, the development or revision of writing systems, or problems of widespread illiteracy.

Björn Jernudd, in taking exception to this state of affairs, suggests that language planning should not continue to be limited to the developing nations since many questions of language planning may as well concern the developed nations, and that language planning efforts should recognize language as a societal resource. [10] Others, such as Das Gupta and Karam, recognize language planning as only one area

of national planning--one which must be viewed in the context of the
political, economic, scientific, social, cultural, and religious situation.

I believe that the language planning needs of a developed country
like the United States are different in kind, at least in part, from
problems many newly emerging nations are experiencing. The United
States is typified by a highly sophisticated and complex network of
international relations; a country which has bilateral and multilateral
interlocking treaties and ties with almost every nation of the world--
military, political, and cultural--and with all of the responsibilities
and obligations this entails; with an economy deeply linked with the
balance of world trade; and with a restless, pluralistic society facing
an identity crisis from within--to melt or not to melt--and from without the challenge to live in an increasingly interactive and inter-
affective world.

Language can be viewed as a linguistic system and as a tool. One
can plan language or its use. From a functional point of view language can be seen as a commodity. John Hoffman has recently noted
that

> ... language is so much taken for granted that its resemblance
> to other consumer goods often goes unnoticed. Yet, in several
> important respects, languages are produced, conveyed, and
> consumed much like any other product. In the flow of language,
> just as in the flow of goods, there are critical points at which
> problems arise to be identified, analyzed and explained. [11]

Language planning, in a context of foreign language education, can
view language as a product--a linguistic system through which the
common ideals, fears, and hopes of a community of men are shared.
Between four and five million Americans consumed a language last
year. A kind of language planning that is needed is one that will help
establish a more reliable delivery system for those languages, and
will deliver the right language in the right amount, at the right time,
to the right people, and for the right reason.

In an interest group session of the Georgetown University Round
Table on Languages and Linguistics 1973, I outlined the need for a
resources-oriented language planning typology. [12] Such a typology
would permit (1) focus on the identification of the product/problem
(i. e. which language or languages need to be learned/taught); (2) focus
on the development of a data base by which to determine supply and
demand needs over a long-range period: appropriate criteria for this
task would include diplomatic and political considerations, business,
industry, and commerce (including foreign trade and multinational
corporations), as well as the needs in government, education, and the

arts and humanities; (3) focus on the specification of the physical resources necessary to accomplish the task in light of the product and
projected human resource needs; and (4) focus on the development of
the delivery system best capable of achieving the goals, with an effective ongoing evaluation or monitoring system.

Joshua Fishman, in a recent state-of-the-art paper on language
planning and language planning research, criticizes the two fields for
being too loosely joined.

Language planning research has, increasingly, been studying
language planning practice, i. e. decision-making in connection
with language problems. However, the practitioners of language planning (legislators, implementors of policy, government agencies and language academy personnel, language
specialists in private industry, etc.) have not yet turned to
or utilized language planning research to any major degree
as a guide to their own procedures. 13

This criticism by Fishman underscores the importance for the
language planning researchers to provide additional models and research more relevant to the broader needs of the language planning
practitioners in this country.

A positive and practical step in the right direction would be joint
discussions of the two groups focusing on the following areas.

(1) The creation of a greater awareness that language planning is
necessary. In a decentralized education system such as ours,
responsibility for decision-making is found in many agencies and
organizations at the national, state, and local levels. The need for
awareness extends to the public as well. Those responsible for making decisions must understand why planning will help them make better
decisions, and when and how to use it.

(2) The identification of a framework within which planning agencies,
organizations, and individuals may cooperatively develop a comprehensive and clearly enunciated national language planning effort.

2. A brief historical sketch. A brief historical review of some
of the more informal examples of language planning efforts of the
sort I am talking about today reveals that more language planning
is taking place in this country than we might at first realize. Some
of the institutions that have played important roles include the
following.

(1) Education associations such as the Modern Language Association
of America, the American Council on the Teaching of Foreign Languages, the Center for Applied Linguistics, all of the AATs, the language committees of the various area associations, the American

Council on Education, the Social Science Research Council and the American Council of Learned Societies, and the hundreds of state and local professional groups and associations of language teachers who annually meet to share teaching strategies, worry about dwindling enrollments, and plan for new student career objectives.

(2) The various federal and state agencies with a concern for language are of two types. The first type includes the mission-oriented agencies (i. e. those who require language-proficient personnel to carry out their agency mandate), such as the Foreign Service Institute of the Department of State, the National Security Agency, the Central Intelligence Agency, the Defense Language Institute, the United States Information Agency, the Peace Corps, and numerous other agencies one normally does not associate with a need for language-skilled personnel such as the FBI, the Census Bureau, the Smithsonian Institution, Immigration and Naturalization, the Bureau of Place Names, the Library of Congress, Agriculture, and many more. The state departments of education and local education associations also belong in this category.

The second type of agency concerned with language development includes such agencies as the U. S. Office of Education, the National Endowment for the Humanities, the National Science Foundation, and the Department of State in its responsibility for the administration of a large part of the Fulbright-Hays programs. These agencies have a responsibility for the management of public funds appropriated under authorizing legislations by the Congress of the United States. These funds are in support of training programs or research at schools, colleges, and universities, and other eligible organizations.

Those institutions which exercise an authorizing, overseeing, and monitoring function in our society are institutions such as the United States Congress, the General Accounting Office, the Office of Management and Budget, and their counterparts at the state and local levels.

The various foundations which provide assistance to language development are institutions such as the Ford, Carnegie, Mellon, and Rockefeller Foundations, as well as foundations set up by foreign governments to encourage the study of the language and culture of the nation they represent.

The entire language community is represented by local schools, colleges, and universities, through the language training curricula they have developed and the research they have conducted.

All of the above agencies, organizations, and educational institutions constitute the language planning capability of the United States, a formidable body of professional expertise and experience indeed, charged with a responsibility for the administration of nearly one billion dollars worth of foreign language training and research activities annually. Would not a carefully developed framework for

the systematic coordination of language and language planning resources make an important contribution to our national language
planning efforts?

3. Language planning for the future of foreign language study in
the United States. The third area for profitable mutual discussion
between language planning researchers and practitioners is in the joint
development of an operational plan. A detailed outline of such a plan
is well beyond the scope of this presentation; yet its basic steps would
include: (1) a preliminary identification of suspected problem areas
(in other words, what is to be planned); (2) the collection of data; (3)
the refinement of the problems identified based upon the data col-
lected; (4) the development of alternative solutions to the problems;
(5) the selection of a solution which then becomes a policy decision;
and (6) the delivery system begins the process of implementation.

Even the briefest historical sketch of the language planning efforts
in the United States would be well beyond the constraints of this paper.
Let me rather illustrate my point by a few examples.

If one looks at the history of the rise (and fall) of foreign language
enrollments in the public school system since 1890 (the first year for
which we have data), one notices some rather clear trends.[14]

Around the year 1900, language study in the schools for all
practical purposes meant Latin (50% at its highest point) and modern
foreign languages (approximately 25%). As World War I grew closer,
the enrollments shifted and by 1915 there was a nearly even split
(35% each). Were we preparing subconsciously to join the modern
world? After World War I, enrollments declined in both languages
and by 1922 were 27% each. It is interesting to note that in 1934, in
the midst of the Great Depression, the combined figure for Latin and
modern foreign languages was 27%. In 1974, that combined figure
was 24%. Latin went into a permanent decline while modern foreign
languages rose and fell. From 1934 to 1948 the enrollments declined
to 13%, and by 1958 had grown only to 16%. If enrollments grew prior
to World War I, why did they decline prior to and during World War
II? Were we doing our best talking out of the mouth of a gun?

Sputnik may have had a skyrocket effect on foreign language study
in the United States. Unfortunately, there are no figures for 1957, but
by 1958 enrollments grew to 16%, and to 19% in 1959. We then saw a
gradual growth, as NDEA funds began to reach the field, up to a peak
of almost 28% by 1968. We are now in a decline.

Let us look at the enrollments in higher education for a moment.
Early statistics are unfortunately hard to get, and there is no data
for 1957. However, if we look at all languages we see a growth of
approximately 14% from 1958-59. In selected languages, however,
it was much higher: Russian 56%, Chinese 45%, and Japanese 42%.

Today, Russian has leveled off and had declined 20% since 1968. The other lesser taught languages, however, still show a modest rise overall. Is the skyrocket coming down?

What does all of this have to do with language planning? If one looks at enrollment trends, growth and decline appear to be tied in with external events--events that are largely uncontrollable and unpredictable. In fact, if you trace languages like Chinese and Arabic, you can fix growth spurts with the development of the Chinese atomic bomb and the Nixon visit, or the emergence of the oil crisis.

Is this to be the future of foreign language study in the United States--post factum responses to external events wholly beyond our ability to predict and plan for?

Things are not as bad as they may seem. Language planning is going on. In the 1920s the Carnegie Corporation financed a study of foreign languages. The report concluded that reading was the only attainable objective in public secondary schools and this became our national policy until World War II. World War II itself provided the impetus for one of the best coordinated planning efforts for language in the history of the country. The American Council of Learned Societies (ACLS) in 1941 cooperated with the military to establish an intensive language program which led to the development of the foreign area and language studies program of the Army Specialized Training Program. Following World War II, the Ford Foundation funded the Committee on Language Program of the ACLS and a major Program in Oriental Languages was launched in 1952.

Bill Shaefer has pointed out that 25 years ago, in 1952, the Modern Language Association (MLA) inaugurated its Foreign Language Program aided by the Rockefeller Foundation, and in 1956 issued a nine-point policy statement. In 1957 MLA initiated a five-year plan which resulted in the establishment of the Center for Applied Linguistics, with support from the Ford Foundation. All of the planning and experience of all those programs prepared this country to respond to Sputnik. The fabric out of which NDEA was woven came primarily from the separate threads of the several concerned programs and interests that had represented both the commonly and uncommonly taught languages in the post-World War II period.

Another example of current language planning is represented by the Interagency Language Roundtable--an informal group of Federal agencies that meet regularly to plan and coordinate the language training and research needs of the mission-oriented agencies for foreign language personnel. Some language planning is going on.

What are some of the implications of language planning for the future of foreign language study in the United States? There are several very obvious ones.

(1) There would be less duplication of effort and increased cooperation between all of the constituencies responsible for foreign language education.

(2) There would be an enhanced national capability to better match our supply with our demand.

(3) The selection of alternative approaches to the teaching of foreign languages (either teaching strategies or the social organization of language teaching) would be based on firmer evidence.

(4) Scarce resources could be focused on more linguistically productive avenues.

(5) Decision-making could be taken out of the political or popular arenas.

Charles Ferguson asked the question: what is our American language policy? I agree with him that there is an implicit policy which has yet to be articulated. It is time to provide a better framework for our national language planning efforts.

It is the hope of many citizens and language specialists that the good efforts of Mr. Simon, Mr. Panetta, and Mr. Tsongas toward the establishment of a Presidential Commission may help the nation to focus better on the important role that language plays in an interdependent world and may provide the impetus, two decades after Sputnik, to help make our national language policy more explicit.

NOTES

This article was written by Richard T. Thompson in his private capacity. No official support or endorsement by the United States Office of Education is intended or should be inferred.

1. The Washington Star, October 4, 1977, p. 1.

2. Ibid.

3. See p. 1 of CSIS Monograph, Georgetown University (February, 1977).

4. Shirley Brice Heath. 1977. Language and politics in the United States. In: Georgetown University Round Table on Languages and Linguistics 1977. Edited by Muriel Saville-Troike. Washington, D.C.: Georgetown University Press. 271.

5. Ibid.

6. See Language and Development: A Retrospective Survey of Ford Foundation Language Projects 1952-1974, Vol. 1. 1975.

7. Ward, op. cit., p. 2.

8. See p. 3. Published by the International Education Project, American Council on Education, One Dupont Circle, Washington, D.C. (October, 1975).

9. References for Students of Language Planning, East-West Culture Learning Institute, Honolulu (April, 1977).

10. Björn H. Jernudd. 1973. Language planning as a type of language treatment. In: Language planning: Current issues and research. Edited by Joan Rubin and Roger W. Shuy. Washington, D. C.: Georgetown University Press. 11-23.

11. 'The prediction of success in language planning', The International Journal of the Sociology of Language, Vol. 1 (1974), p. 39.

12. Richard T. Thompson. 1973. Language resources and the national interest. In: Georgetown University Round Table on Languages and Linguistics 1973. Edited by Kurt R. Jankowsky. Washington, D. C.: Georgetown University Press. 225-231.

13. 'Language Planning and Language Planning Research: The State of the Art.' In: Advances in Language Planning. Edited by Joshua Fishman, 1974. The Hague: Mouton. 15.

14. The data on registrations are drawn from the periodic surveys conducted by The Modern Language Association and The American Council on the Teaching of Foreign Languages.

FOURTH PLENARY SESSION
INTRODUCTION

JAMES E. ALATIS
Dean, School of Languages and Linguistics
Georgetown University

Good morning, ladies and gentlemen.
Welcome to the fourth and final plenary session of this conference
on language in American life.
Our main speaker this morning is Dr. S. Frederick Starr. Dr.
Starr took his B. A. at Yale in 1962 in Classics and Ancient History,
his M. A. at Cambridge University in Slavonic Languages, and his
Ph. D. at Princeton in Russian History. He has been professor of
Russian History at Princeton, and in 1975 became secretary of the
Kennan Institute for Advanced Russian Studies at the Woodrow Wilson
Center of the Smithsonian Institution.
Dr. Starr's paper will be followed by a discussion on 'The foreign
language teaching profession at the crossroads' led by Richard Barrutia
of the University of California at Irvine who is currently president of
the AATSP, Richard I. Brod of the Modern Language Association, and
Rose Hayden, Director of the International Education Project of the
American Council on Education.
It is a great pleasure to present to you Dr. Starr, who will speak
to us on 'Why not "international high schools?"'.

WHY NOT 'INTERNATIONAL HIGH SCHOOLS'?

S. FREDERICK STARR
Secretary, Kennan Institute
for Advanced Russian Studies,
Woodrow Wilson International Center for Scholars

Massive evidence has recently been brought forward to demonstrate that foreign languages and international studies should be promoted at every level of our educational system. Robert E. Ward summarized the case in his essay on <u>National Needs for International Education</u> and I find myself in emphatic agreement with nearly every point he makes. The only problem is that the argument from need has failed to convince many of those people to whom it is addressed, not merely because some of the latter group may be immune to reason, as some may feel, but also because the argument is far more effective with regard to international studies generally than for the specific issue of language training. After all, it is asserted, if we have managed to carry out $203 billion of foreign trade each year with scant recourse to foreign languages, why should we change?

We should change, if only for the simple reason that the present position of English in the world is bound to be eroded somewhat by the rise of linguistic nationalism, and that the claims of such linguistic pride are hard to resist when we are dependent upon commodities controlled by the bearers of such pride. But will this ever lead to the widespread study of Arabic, Hindi, Swahili, Japanese, Russian, and numerous other 'critical languages' at schools across the land? I see little likelihood that it will. Now if this is the case, then those who would argue that all our linguistic needs can be met with a single drive for more language study are in error. Clearly, massive programs will be needed if every American child is to have the opportunity to study a major foreign language under competent teachers, the

127

way he can now learn basic mathematics and reading. But equally clearly, the national need for persons trained in the more exotic languages must be met through much smaller and more closely targeted programs of instruction than those which introduce students to the major languages of learning and world commerce.

Were we conforming to the historical evolution of this discussion, we should at this point turn to the universities and ask them to provide the requisite number of specialists trained in exotic languages. A review of the history of Title VI programs shows that much has been done at the undergraduate and especially at the graduate levels over the years to promote this end. Such programs should continue, of course, but they are not without serious faults. For like all language training at the university level, these programs come too late in the curriculum and rarely develop in the student a first-class competence in the given language. How else, then, might such skills be developed? The answer that I would like to propose today is to shift the center of activity from the universities to the grade schools and high schools, and in particular to special 'International High Schools' that would be created within large urban school districts. Such schools, I believe, offer the most promising means of meeting the national need for persons with high competence in foreign languages.

What would the curriculum of such schools consist of? First, they would meet the standard state requirements in all fields. But just as the Bronx High School of Science places a relatively strong emphasis on courses in the natural sciences, and just as the high schools of the arts in Washington, Cincinnati, New York, and elsewhere devote special attention to the visual arts, music, and drama, so would an International High School underscore foreign languages, which would be taught with great intensity and would be used, for the more advanced students, as a medium of instruction, as well. Such a school would give students a strong command of one foreign language and a solid introduction to a second. If the first language would normally be one of the more commonly taught tongues, the second might be one of several of the 'critical languages' for which there is, or will be, a particular national need.

I have spoken of the many existing special high schools of the arts and of the sciences as obvious models for the International High Schools which I advocate. Besides these, one might speak of the several European countries which have actually established such institutions. The Russian 'Internat' schools and certain German gymnasia are offering intensive courses in language and area studies, over and above the impressive language training common to their school systems as a whole.

The one school in the United States that comes closest to what I have in mind is The International School in Washington, D. C. Founded 12 years ago by Dorothy Goodman, a pedagogue of great vision and energy, the institution was originally established as a grade school but has now been expanded to include all 12 grades. Some graduates choose to continue their language work in their subsequent studies and even to build their careers around them. All find themselves in a relatively favored position in the college admissions sweepstakes. Whatever they choose to do, these young people are given linguistic tools that our world increasingly values.

It might be argued that the schools I am proposing are ill suited to our public educational system. But far from being inappropriate for the multi-ethnic conditions of our large cities, such schools could build on existing bilingualism far more effectively than most current programs directed toward such communities. Thus, if 40 percent of a student body arrives in the International High School knowing Spanish, they could devote themselves to English and just one other foreign language--possibly another Romance language but, just as likely, one of the less commonly taught 'critical languages'. If a given community includes a large number of Chinese, Greeks, Croatians, or whatever, the language of that minority could meet one of the two requirements, leaving students from such families free to concentrate on their second language, be it French, Russian, or Spanish. An International High School would accept only those students who are genuinely interested in its curriculum, but it would be a great leveller, building equally on the strengths of native-born Americans and immigrants. Thanks to the diversity of our ethnic makeup, the nation's International High Schools as a group would the more easily become laboratories for linguistic expertise in many languages currently neglected.

It may be objected that these are distinctly inauspicious times for founding new schools when so many old ones are being closed for lack of students. Quite the contrary. As we learned in the 1950s and the 1960s, expanding school systems are peculiarly conservative in many respects. Precisely when a system is forced to contract is it best able to make bold decisions as to what special areas it wishes to emphasize and to redirect part of the remaining schools and resources into those areas.

Such conditions have already given rise to numerous innovations throughout the country, including the establishment of 'magnet schools' of various types. Such schools, in Buffalo and elsewhere, are not only providing pupils (and their parents) with the possibility of choice in the focus of their education, but in a way that overcomes the narrow bounds of neighborhoods and groups. The time is ripe, then, to place International High Schools on the agenda of big city school boards. When this happens, the administrators should be told not only that such schools will promote a worthy national objective but also that they will do so more efficiently than any other means known. Their efficiency derives from the fact that their integrated curricula would provide types of reinforcement for language study far surpassing what would be possible in the usual high school programs.

This question of effectiveness is crucial. Various states have published lists of the 'exotic' languages being offered in their primary and secondary schools. I would be more impressed if they would publish the test scores of the students who have been through such courses, or any other courses. It is of little moment if a school--or university, for that matter--exposes some students to a year or two of Japanese, at two or three hours a week. This may contribute in some general way to what is now termed 'international awareness', but it does not provide the competence that would serve both the student's future and the nation's interest.

I have deliberately avoided the question of federal funding. Since the cost of special high schools in the arts and in the sciences has been borne by large urban systems, there is no reason why International High Schools should not also be locally funded. It may be useful, however, as a means of encouraging the establishment of such schools, for the U.S. Office of Education to make available funds to cover the cost of planning and development. This could readily be accomplished through Section 603 of Title VI of the National Defense Education Act, which provides funds for the widest variety of projects promoting international awareness in the schools.

Lest this discussion conclude on too narrowly utilitarian a note, permit me to turn in closing to the ideal of a liberal education. The fact that a conference is being devoted to the teaching of foreign languages and that the conference is considering the issue in the context of national need is an innovation. As you know, it was long assumed that intensive training in a classical tongue or in one of the two or three major European languages was inherently a part of a good education. So obvious was this that few thought it necessary to defend the proposition. When the attack came--as it did, for instance, when Thomas Huxley raised the banner of natural science against Matthew Arnold's 'literary' education--the subsequent defense was couched in broadly philosophical terms embracing the humanities as a whole, rather than languages specifically. Had Arnold mounted any special defense of language study, it would certainly not have been couched in any pragmatic terms, such as the national need. Like most people in our own day, he would have assented to Cardinal Newman's assertion that 'liberal knowledge is its own end'.

It is true that an International High School would promote the national interest, just as it would equip students with practical tools for the future in a way that existing programs cannot pretend to do. But it would also be at least as hospitable a setting for humanistic education in the classical sense as anything existing today. In the last analysis, how much would such a school differ from the many publicly and privately funded Latin schools that once existed throughout our country? Language would be the core of the curriculum but would simultaneously serve as the avenue through which the student would confront major civilizations and, through that confrontation, come to know better his own world and himself. In this sense, an International High School, while meeting a national need, would give the student an education that would be its own reward.

One need not choose between meeting a national need and fostering these most noble ideals of education. As A. Whitney Griswold wrote back in the 1950s when he was president of Yale, it is possible to have 'better men and better mousetraps'.

THE FOREIGN LANGUAGE TEACHING PROFESSION AT THE CROSSROADS

RICHARD BARRUTIA
University of California, Irvine

Although this paper bears the title of the conference theme, the particular crossroads I have decided to discuss here concerns foreign language teaching methodology. This leads then, to the tongue-in-cheek subtitle: 'The principal actors in the obstruction of <u>active</u> language learning may have been the linguists'. During the last three decades we have seen pedagogical changes in our field appear with accelerated frequency. Just as in all arts, resources and needs change and the heresy of one generation is the orthodoxy of the next.

Let us start by getting some of the already crossed historical roads behind us. In the past, they would come up after periods of hundreds of years, as shown in an important book by Kelly (1974).

Period		Characteristics	Values and goals
1,000 years	Classic	communicative action	orators with impeccable control
	Dark Ages	contemplative, meditative	philosophy and analytic studies
	Renaissance	action, communication	spontaneous practice and active teaching
300 years	Age of Reason	meditation and contemplation	theory, philosophy of grammar, Cartesian logic
	Modern	action, communication	return to practice with variations

The great language teacher Comenius, who switched his active Renaissance-style teaching to that of systems governed by grammatical principles, was already foreshadowing the seventeenth century. By then the primary discipline was Cartesian logic that attempted to relate everything to a single logic model. Where language is concerned this implies that all languages stem from one basic grammar that could be deduced from the mother tongue. According to Kelly, it is to this notion that we owe the development of the grammar translation method.

Now let us look at a more recent set of crossroads.

Period	Method
End of nineteenth century	'Natural'
Beginning of twentieth century	Grammar translation
1925–1940	Direct
1940–1950	Grammar translation
1950–1970	Audio lingual
1970–1980	Eclectic?
1980–?	'Natural'

The swings of the pendulum show a return to cognitive practices when the sociohistoric milieu is in a thinking stage and because seductive linguistic theories seem to promise a lot for nonlinguist foreign language teachers.

One could list three major goals in foreign language teaching: (1) literary-artistic, (2) social, (3) theoretical-philosophical. The artistic literary goal demands appreciation of art as well as its creation. The social goal concerns behavioristic aspects of communication. The philosophical theory goal requires analysis and it is here that linguistics is sometimes confused with the teaching of languages (Kelly 1974).

On reviewing the most recent research reports concerning second language acquisition, we find a continuation of the cyclic evolution as observed by Kelly. It reveals an alternation between the social and philosophical aims of language teaching, with the literary aim acting as a balance. On closer study of this literature one cannot avoid the unfortunate conclusion that we still know very little about learning in general, and, based on empirical studies, very little about the patterns, processes, taxonomies, or hierarchical features of second language acquisition specifically. The research reveals four major types of analysis: (1) contrastive analysis, (2) error analysis, (3) performance analysis, and (4) discourse analysis. The bottom line of the studies concerning these various modes all lead to a dead end as far as a productive and empirically proven teaching methodology is concerned. The findings of Hakuta and Cancino (1977) in a capsulized version, show the following. (1) Contrastive analysis: 'Moreover, learners did not in fact make all the errors predicted by contrastive analysis (Nickel 1971; Stockwell, Bowen, and Martin 1965). When the inadequacy of contrastive analysis as a predictive model became apparent, Wardhaugh (1970) drew the useful distinction between strong and weak versions of the approach. The strong version claimed to predict errors, while the weak version simply accounted for errors that occurred. Contrastive analysis survives only in its weak form with an obvious shortcoming; it gives an incomplete representation of the second language acquisition process since it can account only for some, not all, of the errors. Recently it has been incorporated into the more general approach of error analysis (Schumann and Stenson 1975), which analyzes all systematic deviations of the learner's language from the target language norms.' (2) Error analysis: 'Contrastive analysis was, in effect, consumed by error analysis because the evidence of interference errors it used failed to account for the learner's noninterference errors. Along similar lines, error analysis does not appear to provide a methodology with adequate sensitivity to detect phenomena such as structural avoidance. With increasing sophistication in the methods available to infer knowledge from performance, error analysis is currently in the process of being incorporated within an attempt to describe the learner's overall performance, not necessarily restricting the scope of analysis to errors alone. This line of work (Svartvik 1973), once again bears the marks of work in first-language acquisition.' (3) Performance analysis: 'Although Fillmore's examples are provocative, the principles used by the learner to analyze the prefabricated forms need to be specified; the traditional problem of the emergence of syntax remains to be solved.' Finally, (4) Discourse analysis: 'Implicit in studies of discourse is the importance of input. Unfortunately, rigorous empirical studies of the characteristics of input to the learner are nowhere to be seen in the second language literature.'

In a seminal article by Stratton (1977), a strong case is made for 'Putting the Communicative Syllabus in Its Place', but the multifunctional nature of all speech acts finally mitigates against her major objective. Robinson (1972) states that because of the nature of language and human behavior and the desire to generalize, all such taxonomies will inevitably be inadequate.

We continue to treat the art of teaching and the miracle of language as if they were 'merely' a science. We have seen how human languages have resisted with an unexpected tenacity every attempt to dehumanize or reduce them to technology. Chiseling them in stone did not freeze language, and neither did the Gutenburg press; nor will the computer reduce this living stuff to a cold formula. Why have language patterns for MT or for communicative syllabus been so hard to pin down? There are many reasons, but one of the main ones might be something that has been treated only briefly in linguistic literature. This element is the multifunctional nature of all utterances. Perhaps we should ask ourselves: What is the most difficult kind of pattern to find and describe or label? It may be the nonpattern, the arbitrary or random, totally unpredictable arrangement that is the most elusive to discover. I mention this not in connection with structural nor GT grammar, but rather in connection with recent attempts by linguists to make a taxonomy of language patterns for a communicative syllabus for second language acquisition purposes.

It seems clear that speech acts are sociocultural and historic-situational units of behavior, and as such are totally unpredictable. Though we do not forget the speech act itself which is in the long-term memory to be used again, the multifunctional nature of the speech act is totally forgettable resulting to the short-term memory. Isn't it marvelous that we have a memory and isn't it equally marvelous that we have a memory release that we can forget? If it were not for forgetting, we would be like the computers that cannot know what is unimportant enough to forget. It would be better if libraries had a self-destruct mechanism in the millions of insignificant books on our shelves. It is not at all far fetched to consider that we should learn grammar only in order to forget it, since the pattern for learning speech act sequences may be that there is no pattern and it may be that we cannot come up with a complete theory of language for a peda-gogical grammar. Is it so bad then not to have a theory? For prag-matic purposes it is preferable to have good practices in FL teaching with incomplete theories than vice versa. If FL teaching is an art, and history shows that it is, we should not be afraid of intuitive in-spiration and practices that work, regardless of how well they fit into linguistic theories. Painters, writers, musicians, actors know, if it works, do it. For thousands of years the healing art of acupuncture has been an effective tool and only now are the underlying theories being sought. The miracle of learning language, the most complex of all man's activities, probably has more difficult theoretical under-pinnings than acupuncture or even than the structure and behavior of DNA. So it seems that we should not be too concerned about in-complete theories but rather we should be diligent in finding workable theories--and above all, not misuse them as has sometimes been done in the past.

Now I come to the final crossroad. I know that it is dangerous to make predictions and one should never do it, especially before such a professional audience as this. But the swing of the pendulum, the times we live in, the historical cyclical nature of shifts in methodology, and the evidence from our experiments at the University of California-Irvine lead me to throw caution to the winds.

I believe that FL teaching of the future shall recognize these principles that we have not recognized in the past: (1) that the humanistic art of language teaching and the miracle of language learning are greater than the distilled theories that underlie any of their parts; (2) that specific taxonomies need not be our main concern because they would be unpredictable if the learning were free.

I believe these principles will be manifest by the practice of the following methodologies in beginning language classrooms: (1) classroom time devoted to communication practice only; (2) never let explanations, repetitions, etc. interfere with communication practice; (3) never do pattern drills in class that are not exactly like real and logical communications; (4) never change the subject to discussion about language pronunciation, grammar, etc.; (5) never correct communication efforts; (6) teacher should never vary from the target language; (7) allow student to use any language or no language to communicate; (8) work on listening comprehension; (9) use the book only as homework for the cognitive skills understanding grammar; (10) do drilling only in the language lab outside of class time; (11) use students' own progress in communicating for the affective domain instead of grades, credits, test scores, and the completion of requirements as motivation.

Following the cycles of time, this approach to language teaching will probably be called once again 'The Natural Method'.

REFERENCES

Hakuta, Kenji, and Herlinda Cancino. 1977. Trends in second-language-acquisition research. Harvard Educational Review 47.3.

Kelly, L. G. 1974. Twenty-five centuries of language teaching 500 B.C.-1969. Rowley, Massachusetts: Newbury House.

Nickel, G. 1971. Problems of learners' difficulties in foreign language acquisition. International Review of Applied Linguistics 9.219-227.

Robinson, W. P. 1972. Language and social behavior. Harmondsworth, England: Penguin.

Schumann, J., and N. Stenson, eds. 1975. New frontiers in second language learning. Rowley, Massachusetts: Newbury House.

Stockwell, R., J. Bowen, and J. Martin. 1965. The grammatical structures of English and Spanish. Chicago: University of Chicago Press.

Stratton, Florence. 1977. Putting the communicative syllabus in its place. TESOL Quarterly 2.2.

Svartvik, J. 1973. Errata: Papers in error analysis. Lund, Sweden: Gleerup.

Wardhaugh, R. 1970. The contrastive analysis hypothesis. TESOL Quarterly 4. 123-130.

THE FOREIGN LANGUAGE TEACHING PROFESSION AT THE CROSSROADS

ROSE HAYDEN
Director, International Education Project,
American Council on Education

I have been asked by our host to try to draw together some of the concepts that we have been addressing at this conference, before we conclude with the presentation, 'A Look at the Profession'. As I said in a previous article, it is a bit like 'nailing jello to the wall'. Nonetheless, here goes.

We started out by hearing some rather dismal facts the other day presented by Congressman Paul Simon on provincialism in this country. While I am not going to read the litany of woe to you again, I will give you one or two illustrations that are more familiar to me, reflecting such parochialisms.

Rumor has it that a small-town reporter for a local newspaper in Michigan was given the assignment of covering a monthly meeting of the school board. This session was, however, far from routine, because the local school district had secured, after much correspondence, a guest speaker all the way from the state capital. The distinguished guest began his speech with, and I quote:

As you know, I have been around a good bit. I have made speeches up in Marquette and down in Livonia. I have been to Grand Rapids and Fowlerville and up in Clare. I have been to meetings in Lansing and Detroit, too, of course, and one thing I have learned--people are pretty much the same the world over!

Lest I be criticized for singling out educators, here are a few dandies that are related to the world of business and high finance.

General Motors was puzzled by the lack of enthusiasm the introduction of its Chevrolet Nova automobile aroused in its Puerto Rican dealer- ships. The reason, it turned out, was rather simple. <u>Nova</u> means star, but when pronounced <u>No va</u> it means 'it doesn't go'. The com- pany quickly changed the car's name to Caribe and it has been selling nicely ever since.

Similarly, the Parker Pen Company once blitzed Latin America with an ad campaign that inadvertently maintained that a new ink would help prevent unwanted pregnancies.

Well, enough of that; provincialisms we know about.

Let me proceed with what I heard yesterday and today, and single out four basic categories. Then we can turn to the final order of business on our agenda. These categories I put together under the general headings: National Needs, Societal Needs, Individual Needs, and Professional Implications.

On our National Needs level, we heard from Dr. Peter Krogh, the Dean of the Georgetown University School of Foreign Service, that the conduct of foreign policy very much reflects our ability to train a cadre of experts who are knowledgeable about other peoples and cultures--a minimal cadre of experts, if you will, for meeting national security needs.

For economic reasons, we require professionals who have a second string to their bow. Thus, although they may be marketing majors or finance majors or clergymen, these professionals have to be able to speak a language or know about other cultures in order to transact business in a very interdependent world.

The argument which has surfaced in connection with questions of translation, is the whole question of how we communicate the most recent advances in scientific knowledge. The fact is that we need the best of all minds, if we are going to solve human problems. Cancer research is going on in the Soviet Union as well as in the United States. To the extent that our scientists do not have access to or cannot read the journals reporting on the latest research results around the world, we are clearly not in any position to share or advance this knowledge.

Finally, we heard about the general public and the need for a sophisticated citizenry in an interdependent world--one capable in a democratic system of saying and doing the right things in difficult political circumstances. Mr. Simon mentioned the Panama Canal issue and the level of ignorant debate that surrounded that particular matter. Mr. Ferguson, our first speaker yesterday morning, out- lined the current situation in terms of 'world languages' and 'national languages', reflecting an implicit policy toward language in this country. He outlined very interesting statistics about world lan- guages, about our own indigenous languages in this country, the so- called 'colonial languages', and ended with a discussion of the

'immigrant languages'. I think the basic message is that there is a
lack of fit between which languages are taught, why, and in which
settings, and a lack of response to training in international languages
that dominate in the world in terms of sheer numbers.

Mr. Harold Allen emphasized the matter of strengthening English as a Foreign Language and our foreign policy history with that
issue. Our federal presence internationally may reflect the decline
of our ability to teach English adequately.

Moreover, we have a new approach to meeting national needs. Our
speaker this morning, Mr. Frederick Starr, asked us to look at
another matter, to give attention to the fact that there is a possibility
for innovation and progress at the secondary school level.

I remember hearing on the radio this morning, in the haze of
getting up, that because of the declining birth rates in this country,
47 schools will be closed in Washington, D. C. Now I do not know
if that means 47 buildings, but the equivalent of 47 schools will be
closed. Indeed, maybe one of those buildings could be turned into
an international high school.

Moving now to 'Societal Needs'--and this came out of some of the
job workshops yesterday--we increasingly know that some jobs will
require linguistic ability in the social services. Social justice and
full participation in our country are quite important. Remember, we
are the fourth largest Spanish-speaking country in the world. One
out of three new Americans today is an immigrant. Finally, we must
recognize the facts of life about the economics of interdependence and
our society's need to compete.

Moving to 'Individual Needs', Wilga Rivers outlined some very
interesting theories about probing the human mind, how we learn,
and how we learn to learn--in this case, how we learn languages.
It is very important also that we participate in society and enrich our
identity. In England about six months ago, my colleagues were calling this 'Rootamania', observing the Alex Haley phenomenon in this
country. In fact, they told me a rather rotten joke at the time: the
rumor over there was that Alex Haley had committed suicide when he
found out that he was adopted. At least he had something to feel
deeply about. Dr. Robert Di Pietro mentioned that only 18 percent
of us can really trace our heritage back to the English monoglot
education.

Let me indicate that I fully agree with Mr. Starr about the need
for a humanistic education. Even if security, compassion, and human
survival are not at issue, other culture learning would be prescribed
as the insulin to counteract what one observer has termed the 'excess
sugar of a diabetic culture'. While Americans are physically overfed
and overweight, we are aesthetically starved. Thrills and violence,

not beauty and reflection, abound in our culture. We are a fretful
and anxious people.

One way to avert a national nervous breakdown--and this is something that has not been brought out at this conference--is to educate
children to be aware of the dazzling diversity of cultural expression
around the world and within our own national borders. Full appreciation of such facets of human existence as music, drama, dance,
costumes, sports, cooking, gardening, religious rites, and literature
is unattainable without an education which opens the mind and culti-
vates taste. It is essential in a postindustrial society to assure our
mental health.

I draw here from Stephen Bailey's book, The Purposes of Education: 'However brief the candle of life may seem when viewed by
the eye of eternity, a life span of 75 to 80 years involves a massive 650, 000 to 700, 000 hours of being, which is a lot of
existence, but not necessarily a lot of being'. Even if you deduct
sleep from this, something close to a half-million waking hours will
be experienced by us. Of these, fewer than 90, 000 hours, or less
than one-fifth of this total will be spent on the job. That is a lot of
reruns of 'Kojak'!

Let me turn to 'Professional Implications' and conclude my over-
view of the conference. Here in Washington, of course, there are
always three claims that should make you suspicious. The first is:
'The check is in the mail'. The second is: 'Of course, I'll respect
you just as much tomorrow morning'. The third is: 'Hello there,
I am from Washington, D. C. and I am here to help you'. I do not
know which of these is most dangerous, but I am here from Washington and I hope that I am here to help you with respect to Mr. Simon's
call for political action. I hope you all listened well when the Congressman said yesterday that he was hoping that you can backstop
and deepen the effectiveness of the proposed Presidential Commission
on Foreign Language and International Studies. There has to be some
effort, on a substantive level, to deliver professional inputs to the
commission. The commission will not have much time or much
money. Furthermore, it has to have some political backing so that
its findings will meet in a very timely way with the appropriation
cycle for the support of international education. This would include,
but would not be limited to, the Fulbright Program, Title VI of the
National Defense Education Act, and the National Endowment for the
Humanities, among others. Harold Cannon of the Endowment also
stressed active and appropriate involvement. He mentioned, with
some dismay, the fact that there were only nine proposals out of
over 170 that specifically dealt with the language area. Consider
also the Fund for the Improvement of Postsecondary Education which

now has a new director who is interested in receiving proposals of
an international or linguistic nature.

Finally, there is a need to shape appropriate local-level attitudes.
This one I do not know how to tackle. I think Fred Starr is correct
when he says that we have to shift a bit to a community emphasis,
to the local school emphasis. We are really swimming upstream.
Many believe that the human mind is a finite sponge, that if you learn
a Spanish verb, this blocks out all ability to learn anything there is
to know about English grammar; or if you tell a student where
Botswana is, clearly he or she will not be instructed in the mysteries
of the history of North Carolina. As long as we are working with a
zero-sum concept of the human mind, we need involvement at the
school level. We must combat the statement that if a traditional
education was good enough for me, it is good enough for you. I pro-
test. I do not think it is good enough for anyone.

Dick Thompson addressed this yesterday when he talked about language planning, or linking schools to national purpose. Planners and
practitioners have very little to say to each other at present.
Efficiency and effectiveness of language training are going to depend
very much on building on cognitive studies and research, on being
a consumer of that research, and on translating it into an appropriate planning action.

Let me conclude now by referring you to an article in Profession
77. I will exert great self-restraint and not quote myself. The
article is entitled 'Linking Language to International Education: Some
Do's and Don'ts'. I think it relates closely to the professional implications that are being discussed here. In essence, it is basically a
call to look at language training and ways of better integrating it on
the campus and in the local environment.

In the hope that these parting jokes will cheer you on a rainy day,
I will share with you a story that I heard the other day. It is a Russian
story, a little crude, but to the point. A Russian peasant was bringing his cows in from the pasture in Siberia in a storm. A little bird
was fluttering along behind the cows, but suddenly got so cold and
frozen that it just fell into the snow. The peasant picked up this poor,
suffering little bird and began to blow on its wings to try to warm it
up. Unhappily, the temperature kept dropping and the peasant became desperate. Just then, one of the cows did what cows are wont
to do, and deposited a steaming hot mass on the ground. The peasant
was desperate and the bird was just about breathing its last. Quickly,
the peasant put the bird in the substance up to its neck. Pretty soon,
two or three minutes later, the peasant was startled when the bird
burst into song, happy to be alive. Just at the moment, out of the
barnyard came a fox who scooped up the bird, wiped if off, and
swallowed it whole. Well, the moral of the story is: the one who

puts you in it may not be your enemy. The one who gets you out of it, may not be your friend. But when you are in it up to your neck, don't sing.

CLOSING REMARKS

JAMES E. ALATIS
Dean, School of Languages and Linguistics
Georgetown University

I should like to conclude with a reminder as to the purposes of this
conference. This conference was entitled 'Language in American Life'.
The final plenary session had as its topics 'Why not "international
high schools?"', a topic upon which Dr. Starr has so eloquently
spoken, and the final discussion is supposed to have centered around
the theme, 'The language teaching profession at the crossroads'. The
overall purpose of this conference was to make the public aware of the
importance of language study and to make students aware of the need
to educate for global interdependence, the importance of which is
emphasized by the Congressional Commission on Security and Cooperation in Europe, the so-called Helsinki Accords. In forming a congressional task force to examine the problem of foreign language and
cultural skills development, Congressman Leon Panetta (D.-Calif.),
who spoke on the first evening of this conference, and his colleague,
Congressman Paul Tsongas (D.-Mass.), have stated:

> The elimination of foreign language requirements for gradu-
> ate and advanced degrees and the high number of United States
> military and diplomatic personnel stationed abroad who do not
> have adequate foreign language and cultural skills to deal ef-
> fectively with local populations are matters that...adversely
> affect our national interest. As our business community seeks
> to expand markets, it is confronted with growing nationalism
> in the Third World particularly, which is often expressed as
> anti-Americanism. Not only does American business lose
> ground in international trade, but this failure to understand
> other languages and cultures reinforces our 'ugly American'

145

image abroad. Our foreign language policy and the acceptance
of United States military personnel stationed abroad are
seriously jeopardized by these language deficiencies.

We are also very much aware of the intention of President Carter
to establish a Presidential Commission on foreign languages and
international studies, and it was partly in anticipation of the establishment of that commission that this conference was called. In addition to establishing the Presidential Commission and the Congressional
Task Force, the Carter administration has recently released a plan
for the reorganization of the State Department and the United States Information Agency. As Rose Hayden has said, rethinking, reform, and
active leadership characterize current reassessment efforts in agencies as diverse as the U.S. Office of Education and the Agency for
International Development. Thus, I would like to reinforce Dr. Hayden's comment that we are indeed at an open moment in our national
history. In the broadest sense we are concerned about language teaching in this country and that done by American citizens abroad. We are
naturally disturbed by the trend, begun in the late 1960s, of eliminating the language requirement from degree programs of institutions of
higher learning, primarily because there has been an inevitable reflex
of deemphasis of language learning in the secondary schools. Thus,
at a time in our history when more Americans than ever before are
going to have to know and use a greater variety of languages, our educational system seems to be backing away from providing them with
the means to do so.

The retention or reinstatement of language requirements at institutions of higher education is one approach toward solving the problem.
Yet it is a difficult matter to specify just what conditions contribute to
successful language learning. I am inclined to support the ideas of
Mortimer Graves, former Executive Secretary of the American Council of Learned Societies, who sometime ago recommended that we provide undergraduates with a kind of sophistication in linguistics while
they are learning a second or third foreign language. This would subsequently enable them to learn many languages on their own. It is
appropriate at a conference such as this one to cite the recent report
by Willard Wirtz and his committee on the decline in SAT scores in
this country. That report indicates that, on the whole, students who
take foreign languages do well on SATs. Their scores indeed have
not declined. The report does not suggest that foreign language study
is the cause for this success, but that there appears to be a very
strong correlation. I should like to emphasize that the teaching and
learning of foreign languages, and of English as a foreign language,
are in the national interest and that they deserve bountiful government
support. This meeting on Language in American Life was not called

in the expectation that participants would conclude that there is no connection between the national interest and foreign languages.

There is indeed great cause for optimism. In the past year there has been a steady progression of events, culminating with this conference, which suggests that there is going to be a renaissance in the foreign languages in this country very soon. We must ride the crest of the wave and do it in unity and with some kind of organization. Among the events to which I refer are the conference sponsored by the Rockefeller Foundation, the MLA, and the ACLS which was held in December on virtually the same topic as ours. Another encouraging event is the establishment of the Modern Language Association's task forces on foreign language study. In this year, language education in the United States appears to be at a point of change in the cycle of expansion and contraction that has marked its history. The language task forces of the Modern Language Association and the American Council of Learned Societies are now engaged in setting goals for the study of language in the United States, and identifying expedient means of achieving those aims. As a profession, we must follow the activities and recommendations of these task forces and support them in a unified, coordinated manner. If the language profession itself is to acquire and maintain the intellectual strength and political power necessary in these troubled times, a new concept of the professional and a new concept of a unified professional entity must be created. Those organizations which use their energies to produce such a unified professional entity will ultimately receive the backing of the majority of teachers, of the American people, and of the government which represents them. But, we must first educate the general public about our profession. We can do so in a number of ways, and it behooves us to make the strongest possible case for language study and take it to the public.

I have indicated earlier that I felt that both foreign language teaching and the teaching of English as a foreign language are in the national interest. I should like to make it clear that when those of us who have taught English as a foreign language professionally make such statements, we are not advocating a 'let 'em learn English' attitude, which some other Americans still take. We are struck by the excellent standards, both of English as a foreign language and other foreign languages in Europe. In Europe and elsewhere, English has gradually become the most important and most widely taught foreign or second language. The so-called Third World countries need a knowledge of English and frequently ask our help in providing instruction. There is also no question that it is in our national interest to satisfy their demand. But we must be careful not to do so in a manner that will cause us to be accused of 'linguistic imperialism'. What we must do is find a way of expanding our teaching of English as a foreign language

without making ourselves vulnerable to charges of cultural aggres-
siveness or of designs to make English the lingua franca of the world.

Those of us who teach English as a foreign language professionally have insisted that it is important for Americans abroad to learn
the language of the country in which they are stationed. This has been
the philosophy, for example, of the Fulbright program, under which
many of us have served as exchange scholars. We have at the same
time insisted that Americans at home, in our schools and colleges,
learn at least one foreign language in order to improve communication
among the peoples of the world. We have always stressed the mutu-
ality of this kind of arrangement, and have been careful to point out
that we did not expect the rest of the world to learn English while we
remained complacently monolingual. We are in favor of foreign language instruction for everyone, and for a good part of the world English is the leading foreign language. As Dr. Harold Allen has mentioned in his talk on 'English and global interdependence', there is a
serious decline in support of English as a foreign language abroad.
Not only are our agencies decreasing their support for such activities,
but there is a real danger that our British colleagues, who have been
carrying the heaviest part of the load, may also have to curtail their
support.

One way that I would suggest to help alleviate the problem that
Dr. Allen disclosed is the establishment of some kind of an American
Council for the Teaching of English Abroad, similar to the British
Council. A long-range solution to this problem, as well as to the
problem of the decline of interest in foreign languages in this country
might well be the establishment of a new semigovernmental agency
somewhat similar to the National Science Foundation--perhaps a
National Language Foundation--which would be able to recruit and
train, as well as make grants for needed research and experimentation. This country spends 20 times as much on health research and 60
times as much on defense research as it does on research in education. It is incomprehensible to me that the most affluent nation in the
history of civilization has not been able to contribute substantially to
such things as, for example, research on the regional, social, and
functional varieties of English. With the help of bright young congressmen such as Leon Panetta and Paul Simon, both of whom we have had
the good fortune of having heard at this conference, as well as their
colleagues in the Congress, it is possible that we might be able to
bring about the kind of support that is needed, particularly for language education. The professional organizations represented at this
meeting, with all the AATs, the Joint National Committee, ACTFL,
the Modern Language Association, represent a constituency of over
100,000 people. There is no more verbal, more articulate group of

people in the world than language people and we should make use of
our tools to influence legislation.

Congressman Simon talked to us about language and national policy.
As Dr. Ferguson reminded us, however, whereas at present the United
States has no comprehensive and explicit policy with respect to language, a number of other nations do have official language policies.
We lack the kind of language planning for the future of language study
in the United States about which Dr. Thompson spoke yesterday. I
should like to support Dr. Ferguson's recommendation that the Presidential Commission, once it is appointed, should devote its energies
toward the formulation of a language policy that will enable this
country to take its proper role in the family of nations. I would like
to emphasize another point made by Dr. Ferguson, namely, that
America is the world leader in quality research on first and second
language acquisition. He hastened to add, however, that it is probably
the world's poorest consumer of that research. This situation, too,
must be reversed if the United States is going to make the kind of indispensable contribution to communication with other nations that is
so urgently needed.

Such policies would immeasurably improve our own foreign language resources and needs both at home and abroad. We must become
attuned to the changes affecting language learning and language teaching, not solely in the United States but throughout the world. Foremost among these changes is the enormous growth of international
communication. This has posed an immediate need for real functional
proficiency in foreign languages. Ironically, despite the general decline in foreign language enrollments in the United States--which, I
am happy to report, seems to have 'bottomed out'--it is quite apparent
that in almost every country in the world far more people are urgently
required to have a much better command of many more languages than
ever before in the history of mankind. But it should be pointed out that
this foreign language demand involves a functional command of language
predominantly for practical applications. Foreign language study must
be reshaped to cope both with the dwindling job market for literary
scholars and with the rising public concern over illiteracy in native as
well as foreign languages. Language teachers are currently faced
with classes made up of students with mixed ability and heterogeneous
educational and social backgrounds, aspirations, and needs. Many of
our best universities are reorganizing language teaching in a way that
will meet the needs of these students in an acceptable and successful
way. While I am confident that there will soon be a renaissance in
foreign language instruction and that there is much room for optimism,
I am at the same time convinced that the foreign language profession
is prepared and equipped to engage in the kind of reformation of language teaching which has also already begun.

We must make certain, however, that the renaissance in foreign language instruction in this country be accompanied by the reformation. We must teach more language and make it more attractive and more effective. Our aim should be to help students achieve a satisfactory command--both speaking and understanding--of the ordinary conversational speech of educated native speakers of the language in question. The development of competence in reading and writing of the language is equally important but we must recognize that this is a separate problem. The point of introducing the written language and the methods of dealing with it vary from language to language. In some cases, work on reading and writing begins almost immediately. In other cases, it must be postponed for months. In the early stages, much attention must be paid to accurate pronunciation, comprehension, and oral fluency. Adequate native-speaker models must be provided for the students to imitate. In the absence of these, books, records, tape recordings, special instruction by linguists, and other aids can play important roles. Special attention must be paid to the application of linguistic science to research in first and second language acquisition and to the translation of such research into practical suggestions and recommendations for teacher training and materials development.

The foreign language teaching profession is engaged in changes in approaches, methodology, and materials. Today the methods of teaching foreign languages are more diverse, more flexible, and more specialized than they were a decade ago. Foreign language teaching is becoming more multidisciplinary in its approach and is increasingly using the discoveries of applied linguistics to improve itself. Specifically, recent developments in the fields of psycholinguistics and sociolinguistics have added much to our knowledge about the teaching and learning of foreign languages.

Some uneasiness has been expressed recently on the part of university faculties concerning the position of literary studies in the curriculum. The place of literature in our language programs must be supported. There is no question that the learning of language in order to study its literature is still at the heart of the discipline and should remain so. Still, I believe we would do well to expand the humanistic emphasis of our literature courses. The emphasis should be shifted from 'language and literature' to 'language and culture', with the stress placed on the country, its people, its customs, and its total way of life. The nature of human linguistic communication in all of its philosophic, social, geographic, and ethnic historical implications can be an exciting humanistic study in itself.

Efforts should be made to develop attractive new courses directed toward the special interests of students in disciplines such as history, economics, sociology, political science, or business administration. Even within the area of the basic communication skills, there is much more that can be done to accommodate immediate goals in order to provide a variety of special interest courses designed to meet the particular needs of students who might want to use certain aspects of language as tools for other studies. This adds a pragmatic value to the humanistic goals. At the graduate level, however, it is clear that literature programs cannot be continued without some kind of external subsidy. Regrettably, it is foreign language literature specialists who are having the most difficult time on the job market; and care must be taken lest we glut the academic market and thus exacerbate the unemployment problems of the nation. At the basic skills level, we must insist upon quality above all else; and in order to assure this, we must be absolutely insistent upon small classes, especially for undergraduate language courses. Anything less is false economy.

Special attention must be given also to the matter of entrance and proficiency examinations in the foreign languages. The relationship of class size to quality instruction is undeniable. Since the so-called 'revolution' in foreign language teaching during the 1940s, there has been general professional agreement that efficient language teaching requires small classes. Traditionally, foreign language instruction emphasized translation of texts and memorization of grammatical rules; and these could be fairly well achieved with large student groups. Since the 1940s and 1950s, however, top priority has been given to the spoken language, and since the 1960s emphasis has also been placed on students' achievement of 'general communicative competence'. It follows that if each student is to have adequate opportunities to imitate the instructor's spoken model and to engage in dialogues and controlled conversation with his fellow students, classes must be considerably smaller than once was the case--or might still be the case in some other academic disciplines. Even in advanced reading and writing courses, the small-class concept applies, for the instructor must be able to work frequently with students on an individual basis. To be sure, there has been some difference of opinion on exactly how small a 'small' class must be to enable students to master a language at a fairly rapid pace. Twenty-five years ago, E. V. Gattenby, a leading British foreign language specialist, wrote that 'the pace slows down if there are more than 10 adults or 20 children to one teacher'. Though many would still accept Gattenby's formula, most real teaching situations require some compromise between the ideal and the practicable. One such compromise is to alternate between total-group hours under a senior staff member and small-group sessions under 'drill masters' who may be graduate students or junior instructors. This may appear inefficient in terms of cost and personnel. However, 25 years of professional experience

has shown that, in fact, such classes pay off in the long run by allowing more rapid learning leading to a higher level of individual achievement.

Class size relates also to the total quantity of time allocated for
organized instruction and its rate of intensity as well as the overall
duration of courses. It is a truism among experienced foreign language teachers that an increase in the intensity of teaching leads to a
more than proportionate increase in the rate of learning per unit of
time. There seems to be a lower unit of about 5 to 6 hours a week below which the learning yield per hour drops off drastically. In other
words, rates of achievement are improved by higher rates of intensity
in teaching and learning. Quality instruction also presupposes well-
trained native speaking teachers, supervision by trained linguists,
materials which are linguistically sophisticated and pedagogically
sound, and the use of the most modern audio-visual equipment. Admittedly, academic institutions cannot be expected to replicate the
conditions which exist at such institutions as the Department of State's
excellent Foreign Service Institute. Yet, I believe that semi-intensive
courses with classes meeting at least 5 hours a week, including com-
mensurate time devoted to language laboratory and drill, homework,
and extracurricular language activities, are feasible.

I also believe that some kind of minimum standard proficiency
scale similar to that used by the Foreign Service Institute should be
adopted not so much on the basis of academic grades but on the basis
of absolute levels of reading and speaking proficiency. Some might
argue that this would require the establishment of an extensive battery
of standardized tests, which is frequently very expensive. However,
structured oral interview procedures similar to those used by FSI,
while admittedly often subjective in nature, could be applied by qualified faculty and controlled by linguistically sophisticated, foreign language department members. Adoption of such procedures is within
the realm of possibility and deserves to be tried. It should be relatively easy to measure an individual's degree of language learning.
As I have indicated, the FSI has developed and perfected scales of
speaking and reading proficiency and has calibrated them with hundreds
of students enrolled in the School's courses. The Defense Language
Institute (DLI) has adopted similar measuring sticks and uses them
widely in evaluating the performance of their trainees.

It behooves the schools and universities of the private sector to
learn about and profit from these experiences in the government
sector. I believe that similar structured evaluation procedures and
standardized proficiency ratings might contribute greatly to solving
the problem of articulation of foreign language instruction among the
various levels, departments, and schools. All other things being
equal, a student should be able to achieve a minimum proficiency

level of S-3, R-3 in four years, assuming no previous knowledge of
the language. For less commonly taught, or 'hard' languages, especially those with complicated writing systems and those whose structures
are at great variance with English, more time would be required. In
any case, it should be remembered, as Dr. Wilga Rivers of Harvard
has told us, that the United States is the only country in the world that
expects its students to master a language in two years. This expectation is absurd. On the other hand, granted time sufficient to achieve
a minimum of functional proficiency, given linguistically sophisticated
materials, modern technical equipment, and excellent native-, or
near-native faculty, appreciable results in communication skills--
and through them knowledge of another culture--can be reasonably
assured. We should stress the fact that knowledge of cultures other
than our own contributes to the broadening of our students' horizons
and mitigates the deleterious effect of parochialism. Further, by
studying other cultures we acquire new perspectives on our own culture. We must strive to get our students and the American public in
general to understand that decisions that we make in this country have
repercussions abroad, and vice versa. We must stop neglecting the
already overneglected, so-called 'uncommonly taught' languages in
which the majority of the world's population conduct their everyday
business.

It should be emphasized that in all our endeavors, quality is more
urgently needed than quantity. Nor should we neglect the important
factor of maintaining foreign language skills once they have been
achieved. Advanced-level oral and composition courses must be
instituted to assist students in maintaining the so-called 'productive'
skills after completion of their lower division courses. In this connection, I would like to point out that small classes do not produce,
ipso facto, quality. In addition, I would recommend that small
classes in language programs be balanced with vigorous efforts to
develop civilization, culture, and field courses that will have a wide
appeal and that can be taught in a large lecture format, thereby creat-
ing more equitable faculty-student ratios. It must be recognized that
quality foreign language education is expensive but we must cease
making academic decisions on the basis of financial considerations
alone. But dropping foreign language requirements in response to
the need for fiscal retrenchment is a very cynical reason, indeed.

As to the teaching of English as a foreign language, every effort
must be made to reinstitute and adequately fund the National Advisory
Council on the Teaching of English as a Foreign Language, as Dr.
Harold Allen has recommended. The ironic prohibition against distribution of the USIA's excellent English Teaching Forum to U. S. residents must be reversed. Further, I thoroughly subscribe to Dr.
Allen's suggestion that a linguistic advisor to the President of the

United States of America is desperately needed. I totally agree with him that we must carry our share of the burden jointly assumed with Great Britain for the teaching of English as a foreign language abroad. Dr. Allen is correct in stating that unless this trend toward diminished support for EFL is reversed, the effectiveness of international communication for peaceful understanding and the establishment of world order are seriously threatened.

We must keep in mind the idea that language studies should begin before adolescence. It has been stated that in the long run the 'problem' of foreign language study can only be solved in the primary school. This idea recognizes the evidence concerning the process of language learning, introducing study of a second language at an age when young people are naturally curious about language, when they have the fewest inhibitions, and when they most easily imitate new sounds and sound patterns. It also recognizes the fact that the greatest natural barrier to international understanding is the unreasonable reaction to 'foreignness' which is often acquired during childhood, but which may be offset by exposure to foreign speech and behavior. Finally, this idea recognizes the fact that real proficiency in the foreign language requires progressive learning over an extended period. There is an urgent need of providing children who have the ability and the desire the opportunity of continued progress in language study into and through junior and senior high school.

A source of encouragement in this area are the recent legal decisions on bilingual education, which stipulate that the mother tongue of members of various ethnic groups, both of immigrant and of indigenous communities, be used in the education of the children of those groups. Foreign languages are getting a good deal of publicity through bilingual education, and we must all strive to support and strengthen it. We must strike out and fight for bilingual education, and prevent such things as the American Institute for Research Report (the AIR report) from defeating it. The AIR report, which is based on poor scholarship and poor research design, should be exposed for what it is.

I would like to conclude these remarks and this conference by referring back to the title of this final plenary session, 'The foreign language teaching profession at the crossroads'. I believe that there is much room for optimism and I agree with Dr. Wilga Rivers when she insists that we consider the word crossroads in an optimistic, rather than a pessimistic, way. As she put it: 'I thought that if you came to crossroads there were full vistas, one behind you that perhaps you enjoy, and at least three others. And, I think that any kind of pessimistic note about crossroads is rather silly.' I agree also with Dr. Rose Hayden, who insisted that we must be prepared. And this was the whole point of calling this conference; that is, to try to draw the attention of the public to the fact that if anything is going to happen, we, as the foreign language teaching profession, must be ready to move forward in the national interest. As William Riley Parker told us over 25 years ago, 'the common sense of mankind recognizes that inability to communicate readily through the medium of language is a barrier to international understanding--and hence to peace.'